■SCHOLASTIC

Journal Activities
That Sharpen Students' Writing

BY J. M. WOLF

New York • Toronto • London • Auckland • Sydney
Mexico City • New Delhi • Hong Kong • Buenos Aires

Teaching *Resources*

Dedication

To Linda: This one's for you, sis!

Acknowledgments

Working on this project taught me that it "takes a village" to write a book and I wish to thank the many people who helped in the writing of this one. Again, a sincere and hearty thanks to Sarah Longhi, my Teaching Resources editor, for her fabulous editorial eye and positive encouragement. Thanks to Kathleen Keating, who said, "Why don't you write a book about journals?" and to my colleagues for letting me use them as test subjects. Thanks also to the girls' support group for late-night laughs. And of course, a big thanks to my fourth graders of the 2002–2003 school year. Once again, you are the reason I am here!

Cover design by Holly Grundon
Interior design and illustration by Alicia Dorn
ISBN: 0-439-48810-9

Contents

Introduction

Why This Book?

Think about the following question. If you were stranded on a desert island and could have only one thing, what would you choose?

Now, answer the same question with an educational twist: If you were put in an empty classroom and told you could have only one teaching tool, what would you choose? For me, it would be easy. I would have to have student journals.

Over the past twelve years, journals have played an instrumental part in my teaching. I use them not only as places for students to explore free writing but also as educational tools, guiding and directing students in their journeys to become writers.

Journals serve as mini–treasure chests, places students can collect writing objects and ideas. They make a fun tool for teaching grammar and the important mechanics of good writing. They serve as valuable instruments for building community within a classroom.

A student journal cover, enthusiastically decorated by its owner.

In my classroom, journals go further than simply being a place where kids write. They are not "just journals," but teaching instruments for me and places of special writing excitement and magic for kids. I can't imagine teaching without them.

How to Use This Book

There are eight chapters in this book. Each is filled with ideas that offer a variety of ways to use journals in the elementary or middle school classroom. Each chapter's activity set helps develop writing skills in an area of the prewriting and drafting stages of writing—from brainstorming to a first-draft story. Each chapter supports but is independent of the other chapters and is designed so that you can use the activities in whatever order works for you.

You will find sections and activities that help students learn and strengthen grammar, help students brainstorm writing ideas, provide ideas for in-school journal field trips, offer lists of writing prompts, introduce guided-writing simulations, and offer resources that include an annotated bibliography and educational Web sites.

All eight chapters are packed with activities that help transform journals into educational tools that help students strengthen skills and get excited about writing.

Organizing and Structuring Journals

There are unlimited ways students and teachers can organize journals. Some variations on the journal format include

✔ Standard single-subject spiral notebooks—these are very portable and fits easily in a student desk or a teacher book bag.

✔ Five- or six-subject notebooks divided into sections—these journals provide a set organizational structure, making it easier for students to file and locate their entries.

✔ Color-coded spiral notebooks for groups of five or six students—these work well for teachers who wish to collect journals on a regular basis without a search-and-sort headache: the "reds" are collected one week, the "yellows" the next, and so on.

✔ Three-ring binders with loose-leaf paper—these add-in journals are perfect for students who like to write extended projects but who may be reluctant to work on more than one project at a time because they don't know how much space they will need. Students write on loose-leaf paper they keep in a folder and add to their binders as they finish. Some teachers have a special place in their room where binders are kept. Others let kids keep them in their desks or lockers.

A simple journal storage system built to fit inside a bookshelf.

1. UNCOVERING WRITING GEMS: BRAINSTORMING ACTIVITIES

All writing begins with an idea. Sometimes writers find "gems," ideas that feel easy to develop into stories or poems. Other times, writers find "diamonds in the rough," ideas that hold great potential but need polishing and development.

As teachers of writing, we have the exciting job of helping students find, mine, and polish their writing ideas into finished writing gems. This begins with helping students create many ideas for both fiction and nonfiction writing projects.

The following section is filled with brainstorming activities to help students think of and define their own writing ideas in both fiction and nonfiction genres. The activities target some of the "stepping-stone" skills of writing, such as character development in fiction. Although they are smaller parts of the big picture of writing, these skills are important. Working on them will help students better transfer these concepts into bigger writing projects.

On the pages that follow, you will find activities that utilize ordinary decks of playing cards, dice, newspapers, and phone books, as well as sets of reproducible cards, all designed to spark many creative writing ideas for students.

Targeted NCTE Standards for Activities and Extensions in This Chapter:

5. Students employ a wide range of strategies as they write and use different writing process elements appropriately to communicate with different audiences for a variety of purposes.

7. Students conduct research on issues and interests by generating ideas and questions, and by posing problems. They gather, evaluate, and synthesize data from a variety of sources (e.g., print and non-print texts, artifacts, people) to communicate their discoveries in ways that suit their purpose and audience.

Full Suit Writing Prompt Mix-Up
Generating ideas for fiction and nonfiction writing

Let students generate writing ideas by using decks of playing cards to add variety and chance to this prewriting activity. Begin by asking students to shuffle individual decks of cards and draw a specified number (usually five cards or fewer). In list form in their journals, guide students to write the number and suit of each card they picked, leaving several inches of space between the numbers.

Using one prompt for each suit that you select from pages 8–9, ask students to list the same number of things for each prompt as the number on their cards. For example, if a student picks the six of hearts, he or she might list six favorite things from his or her bedroom (a hearts suit prompt choice). You can read the prompts from pages 8–9 aloud, photocopy the pages for students, or copy the prompts onto the class board.

Playing-Card Writing Prompt Variations

Instead of drawing cards from different suits, ask students to separate their cards and draw from only one suit. Provide two to three writing prompts for that specific suit.

For a group activity that involves movement, ask students to draw one card from their complete deck and go to a designated corner of the room according to the suit they have drawn. In "suit" groups, encourage students to brainstorm ideas for one writing prompt you provide. Each student records brainstorms in his or her journal. You may wish to determine the number of ideas the group must brainstorm.

Tip!

Early in the year, I have my class create a list of ways writers generate ideas or get "unstuck," including making a thinking web, drawing a picture (about the topic), and making a list. Students keep this list in a place in their journal for reference and we add to it throughout the year as we think of additional writing tools. The topic brainstorming lists that they write in their journals in the first weeks come in handy when students are looking for ideas to create stories, descriptions, poems, or other writing projects.

Where to Go Next: Writing Ideas

Utilize student brainstorming lists as a way to get writing samples throughout the year. Ask students to choose and develop one of their list ideas in the fall, one in the winter, and one in the spring, or monthly. You may wish to assign students to write in a specific genre, such as a story or a descriptive paragraph, or allow students to choose. Encourage strong paragraph development and help students keep track throughout the year of how their writing changes. Have students developed better skills at writing complete sentences throughout the year? Are they using more vivid words? Is their paragraph structure getting stronger? Handy rubrics for tracking such progress can be found in **40 Rubrics & Checklists to Assess Reading and Writing** (Grades 3–6) by Adele Fiderer (Scholastic, 2002).

Full-Suit Writing Prompt Mix-Up

♥ Hearts ♥

List things you like to do in your spare time.

List favorite things from your bedroom (locker, desk, house, etc.).

List favorite (or unfavorite) foods you have eaten.

List famous people you would like to meet.

List special powers or abilities you would enjoy having (invisibility, power to fly, etc.).

♠ Spades ♠

List states, countries, or landmarks you have visited.

List interesting places you'd like to visit (imaginary or real, on Earth or in space).

List things you would like to grow if you could grow anything in the ground (bubble gum, toys, etc.).

Imagine you are stranded on an island. List the things you would want with you from your bedroom.

List things you would enjoy building from sand, mud, or sticks.

♦ Diamonds ♦

In what ways are you wealthy (not in a monetary sense)?

List people you consider to be valuable to you.

What are some things you do well?

List inventions from your daily life that you consider valuable (computer, car, etc.).

What are things you would like to win as a prize?

♣ Clubs ♣

If you were granted wishes, what would you wish for?

In what ways do you consider yourself lucky?

If you had a penny that brought you nothing but good luck for a day, what things would you do?

Who are well-known people (present or past) you would feel lucky to meet?

List things you wish you could change about the world, your state, your town, or your school.

Kings/Queens

What places would make unusual or interesting "kingdoms" (an ice castle, an underground cave, etc.)?

What qualities do you have that would make you a good leader?

If you were in charge of your house, what rules would you set?

If you were in charge of your school, list things you would change.

What are important qualities that a leader of a country should possess?

Jacks

List some of your funny or embarrassing moments.

List your favorite movies or favorite books.

What are some things you like to do for entertainment?

List animals you would like to interview if they could talk for a day.

What actions or laws do you think would make the world a better place?

◆ Mixed Suit ♠

Persuasive Writing Brainstorms

List reasons that your favorite book is better than others you have read.

List reasons why someone you admire should get an award or be recognized as a "great" person.

List reasons why you would choose to have something (toys, CDs, candy, etc.) easily grow from soil.

List reasons why you think one particular place in the world (anyplace you choose!) would be the best place for a birthday party.

♣ Mixed Suit ♥

Persuasive Writing Brainstorms

List reasons kids should save money.

List ways you would make the world a better place if you were given an unlimited amount of money (how would you spend it?).

List reasons you would want to go back in time and witness a specific historical event.

List five or more things you would like to collect and give a reason why each one is worth collecting.

It's Elemental: Story Elements Card Activities
Generating ideas for narrative writing, narrative character development

Make copies of pages 11–12 and cut out Setting, Object, Character, and Plot cards for the activities that follow.

Setting—Object—Character Combinations

Ask students to draw one card each from the setting, object, and character categories and create a story in which all three things are involved. You may wish to require students to include items from the cards as the main parts of the story or let students create stories in which all three items appear but do not necessarily determine the plot line. Reluctant students might first talk out their stories in a group or with a partner before writing it in their journals. Invite students to read their stories in small groups and let others try to identify the three cards that were drawn. For a variation, ask students to also draw a plot card and incorporate the event on the card as the main plot of the story or as a "side" event.

Group Story

Divide the class into groups of three, giving each student in each group one story element card: setting, character, or object. Each student is responsible for the story element on his or her card and must write a brief description of that element in his or her journal. After students have finished their written descriptions, one member of the group draws a plot card. As a group, members combine individual story elements with the plot card idea to create a story. One student acts as the secretary and writes the story as it is developed.

Character Portrait

Ask students to draw one character card (excluding the "baby" and "teenager" cards) and write a description in their journals of this character during three different times in his or her life. Encourage them to divide their journal page in thirds. In each section students should write a short description of the personality and physical appearance of this character as a baby, a teenager, and an adult.

Story Element Discussion

Hold a class discussion about different kinds of books and their focus. For example, some books are more plot driven, meaning the plot is what really makes the book interesting, such as *Holes* by Louis Sachar. Other books are more character driven; it is the characters that really bring the book to life, such as *Because of Winn-Dixie* by Kate DiCamillo. See if students can think of stories in which the setting plays a very important role. In their journals, let students react to the discussion or keep a list of stories that are character, setting, or plot oriented or a list of authors who tend to favor one element in particular in their work.

Story Elements Cards

Setting		Object	
playground	attic	a red scarf	a lollipop stick
forest	farm	an open door	a scribbled note
gym	carnival	a scratched CD	a cereal box
baseball field	abandoned house	a light	a TV remote
cave	pet store	a book with a missing page	a doughnut

Character

a baby	a teenager
an actress	a singer
a writer	a plumber
a scientist	a painter
a cake decorator	a race car driver

Plot

something is stolen	money is missing
someone is lost	two friends argue
a pet is missing	a treasure is found
friends move away from each other	an unusual flower appears in a garden
a mysterious animal is found	a surprise party is planned

Roll 'Em!: List Activities with Dice

Generating ideas for fiction and nonfiction writing, writing ideas in the world

Dice make a great vehicle for helping students generate writing ideas in this journal activity. Begin by choosing three to five prompts from the list on page 14 and write these on the board. Ask students to copy them in their journals or make copies of the page for students to keep in their journals.

For each prompt, roll a die and list the faceup number on the board next to the prompt. For example, if a six is rolled, you might write it next to "things to do on a weekend," which prompts students to list six things they can do on a weekend. When all the numbers have been placed on the board, each should have its own prompt for which students can create lists.

Tip!

Using overhead dice can provide a fun way for all students to see the numbers as they are being rolled. Invite individual students to roll the die on the overhead.

Need a source for overhead dice? See Resources, page 80.

Where to Go Next: Writing Ideas

Encourage students to develop an idea from one of their lists into a speech. Ask them to write a speech that includes an engaging introduction, specific details, and a summary or conclusion statement. You may wish to ask students to write in a persuasive mode (what animal would make the most interesting pet?), an informative mode (this is an interesting place to visit), or an instructive mode (directions for how to use an unusual new invention). Give students the opportunity to present their speeches.

Specify a prompt for students that lends itself well to a compare-and-contrast writing exercise, such as listing "wild animals you'd like to live with for a week" or "new flavors of ice cream to invent." Invite students to write a page comparing two items from their list. Students can illustrate their writing and post their essays around the room.

Great Literature for Brainstorming

The Word Eater by Mary Amato (New York: Holiday House, 2000) is a chapter book about a small worm named Fip who eats words off pages. A young girl finds Fip and discovers that whenever he eats words he makes those things disappear from the world. This book can be a great part of a listing and problem-solving activity. Ask students to create lists of words they would like to make disappear and discuss the consequences these disappearances might create.

List-Writing Prompts

- ✓ things to do on a weekend

- ✓ favorite (or unfavorite) foods

- ✓ things in your room

- ✓ embarrassing moments

- ✓ special abilities or powers you would like to possess

- ✓ jobs or careers you would like to try

- ✓ places (real or imagined) to visit

- ✓ interesting animals to have as pets

- ✓ spare-time activities

- ✓ things you would do if you were in charge of school (or your family, the country, the world, etc.)

- ✓ things you did (or didn't) do over break

- ✓ new kinds of bubble gum, ice cream, or other favorite foods

- ✓ things you would do if you could drive

- ✓ most disgusting kinds of pizza

- ✓ new names for yourself

- ✓ dangerous places you'd like to visit

- ✓ things you worry about

- ✓ presents you've received

- ✓ wild animals you'd like to live with for a week

- ✓ favorite things in your bedroom

- ✓ things you've eaten in the last 24 hours (or things you wish you'd eaten)

- ✓ times you've been happy

- ✓ things you would invent if you could

Telephone-Book Writing Activities

Exploring and developing characterization, descriptive writing, letter writing

Recycle old phone books in a new way by tearing out some of the pages from both the residential white pages and commercial yellow pages for the activities below.

The White Pages: Character Identities

Distribute individual pages from the residential white pages, instructing students to look at names and choose four or five they find interesting. Chosen names will become the basis for character and story ideas. Ask students to respond in their journals to the writing prompts on page 16 to develop a well-rounded character. Then have them use this character to write more developed pieces in the activities below. (Note: It is important to remind students that these are real names of real people and should be handled with respect. If your students live in a small town, you may wish to get old telephone books from another town.)

✓ Invite students to create a story in which their phone-book character is the main character. What kind of adventures, problems, or situations would their character face? Challenge students to create a story in which their character's name is a significant part of the plot.

✓ Ask students to write a letter to their character introducing themselves, then answer the letter as their character writing back and introducing himself or herself.

✓ Let students look through the yellow pages for jobs that might be of interest to their character. Ask students to write a persuasive paragraph explaining why their character would be "right" for a particular job or company.

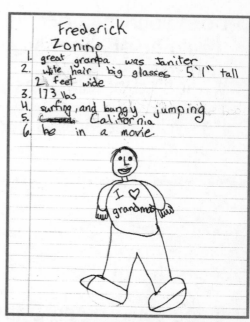

Using a name from the white pages, a student invents characteristics and creates an identity for a story character.

The Yellow Pages: Careers and Business

Ask students to peruse the yellow pages for unusual-sounding companies and jobs. Direct students to list four or five in their journal, pick a favorite, and write a descriptive account of a day in the life as an employee of that company. Use the Yellow Pages section on page 16 to offer students structured prompts.

Phone-Book Prompts

White Pages: Who Am I?

- Create a character identity for the name you've chosen and list his or her hobbies, occupation, age, gender, family, secret wish, favorite food, and place of residence.

- Describe how your character got his or her name. Is he or she named after a relative, a place, or a certain event?

- Does your character "look" like his or her name? If so, list in what ways. In what ways does he or she look different from the name?

- Does your character like his or her name? Why or why not? Would he or she change the name if it were possible?

- What kind of job does your character have?

- Has your character's name influenced him or her in any specific way?

Yellow Pages: What kind of job?

- Does this business or job sound interesting? Why or why not?

- If you could be an employee at this company for one day, what would you do?

- What qualities do you have that would make you suitable for this job?

- If you could be in charge of a company, what company would you choose to run? Why would this be appealing to you? What sorts of things would you do as the boss?

2. THE JOURNAL AS A COLLECTING PLACE

Writers are known collectors. Everything, in the writer's eyes, has the potential to become a story, a poem, or an essay. Consequently, writers are always collecting both things and ideas.

For young writers, journals are an excellent vehicle for collecting. Students can collect not only ideas in journals but also tangible items—objects that can be used for writing ideas and projects.

This section provides writing activities and ideas that feature objects students can collect to glue or tape in their journals. Students can easily find some objects on their own (such as comic strips), while you might provide others. Feathers, pressed leaves, photographs, stickers, and many other items can be paired with ideas for writing prompts in the activities that follow.

Encourage students to bring from home items they feel are special or important and warrant addition to their journals. Including these items makes the journal an inviting and unique place to write. One of my students, for example, clipped in the front of her journal a picture of herself with friends. Photographs such as these, as well as newspaper clippings, feathers, and other things, help make each journal personalized and special to students—and they can serve as writing prompts.

Targeted NCTE Standards for Activities and Extensions in This Chapter:

5. Students employ a wide range of strategies as they write and use different writing process elements appropriately to communicate with different audiences for a variety of purposes.

7. Students conduct research on issues and interests by generating ideas and questions, and by posing problems. They gather, evaluate, and synthesize data from a variety of sources (e.g., print and non-print texts, artifacts, people) to communicate their discoveries in ways that suit their purpose and audience

11. Students participate as knowledgeable, reflective, creative, and critical members of a variety of literacy communities.

12. Students use spoken, written, and visual language to accomplish their own purposes (e.g., for learning, enjoyment, persuasion, and the exchange of information).

Tape-In Treasures

Making real-life writing connections, compare and contrast writing, descriptive writing, narrative writing

Fake Feathers

Dyed feathers come in a variety of striking colors and patterns at craft stores. Provide students with their own feathers (the brighter and stranger the better!) to tape in journals, and offer copies of A Bird of a Feather writing prompts on page 21 for inspiration.

Pretend money

You can collect realistic play money from a variety of sources, including old board games and teacher incentive pads. Or you can purchase play money packets in the toy section of most general stores. Provide each student with a pretend five- or ten-dollar bill to glue or tape in his or her journal. Use the play money as a visual prompt on its own or pair it with the Dollars and Sense writing prompts on page 22.

Pressed Leaves or Flowers

Bring in fallen leaves or allow students to collect leaves or wildflowers (make sure they are not endangered!) from the school grounds. Press the leaves or flowers between pieces of wax paper in phone books or dictionaries and allow them to dry for at least one month. Then let kids glue or tape them in their journals. If possible, provide a microscope for students to study the detailed structures of the leaves and flowers. Have students respond to one of the Flora and Fauna prompts on page 23.

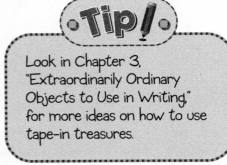

Tip!

Look in Chapter 3, "Extraordinarily Ordinary Objects to Use in Writing," for more ideas on how to use tape-in treasures.

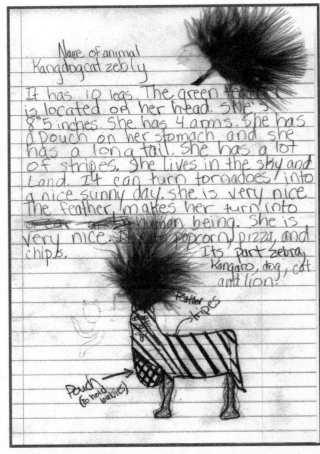

Using dyed feathers and a prompt from page 21, a student describes the imaginary creature "kangdogcat zebly."

Newspapers

There is never a lack of amusing and strange newspaper headlines, particularly in the tabloids. Provide your class with pages from newspapers and ask students to cut out headlines, phrases, or pieces of interesting words they might be able to use in a future story or piece of writing, or for the activities that follow.

✔ Encourage students to bring to class funny or unusual newspaper headlines. Help them create a separate place in their journal to collect such headlines. When a student has a headline to share, write it on the board so that others can add it to their journal collection. Ask students to write their own news story using one of the headlines, or write an imaginary letter to the editor based on the headline.

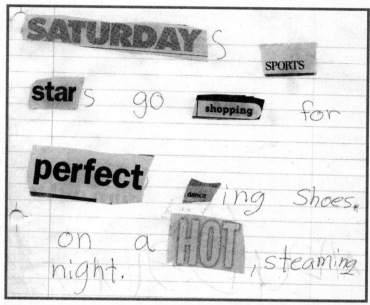

A student combines her own words with words clipped from the newspaper to create an alliterative free-verse poem.

✔ As a poetry activity, have students look through the newspaper and cut out five to ten words or phrases they find interesting. Words may or may not be related. Once students have a collection of phrases, encourage them to place the phrases on a journal page in free-verse form, moving and changing words until they have a poem they like. Encourage students to add written phrases of their own. Once students are satisfied with the arrangement of the words on the page, ask them to glue them in their journals.

✔ Cut out individual words from headlines. Singular nouns and verbs, such as "Earth" and "investigate" work best. Mount the individual clippings on tagboard, laminate for durability, and cut apart. Ask students to assemble in groups of four or five and have each group member pick one or two of the headline words from a bowl or hat. As a group, challenge students to create a fun or funny headline including all of the words they've chosen. Either as a group or as individuals, students then write accompanying news stories that go along with their invented headlines.

Pictures: Magazines, Calendars, Greeting Cards

For these writing activities, collect unwanted catalogs, magazines, calendars, and other items with pictures. Send out a call to parents and colleagues asking for their unwanted catalogs and third-class mail. (Make sure to preview for appropriateness before you put the images out for students to look through.)

Great Literature for Brainstorming

A great read-aloud, **The Landry News** by Andrew Clements (New York: Aladdin Paperbacks, 1999) helps students grasp the power words can have in the world of journalism through the experiences of a young girl who publishes a class newsletter highlighting her thoughts and views about her class. Because of the tone and humor of the story, students are often inspired to create their own class newsletter. Have students brainstorm topics they find important for feature articles and outline lead paragraphs containing the answers to who, what, when, where, why, and how. Then have them do investigative work and finish writing their articles.

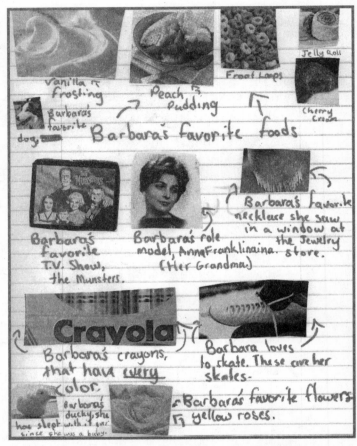

A student writes short descriptions about magazine clippings to illustrate favorite items and meaningful tidbits of personal history associated with her character. (See A Picture and a Thousand Words prompts on page 24.)

In addition to tape-in treasures, you may wish to ask students to reserve a page in their journals to collect titles of books they would like to read, interesting quotes or words they have found, or other small pieces of literary interest that may spark writing ideas. If a student is mentioned in the newspaper for an accomplishment, you may wish to photocopy the article, so everyone can include it in some part of his or her journal.

A Bird of a Feather! Writing Prompts

○ This feather came from an imaginary animal. What is its name? Create an animal that has never before been seen or an animal that is a combination of two or more real animals…but NOT a bird! Write a vivid and detailed description of this animal, making sure to include what it looks like, where it lives, what it eats, and what its daily activities include. If you wish, include an illustration of your animal with your description.

○ Write a story in which your animal is the main character. Try writing from the perspective of the animal or from the perspective of the feather itself. Before you start writing, think about the following things: What is a typical day for this animal? For what, besides flight, does it use its feathers? What kinds of problems does it face? What does it wish for or long for? Are there others of its kind or is it alone? Where does it live and with whom?

○ Think about all of the real or imaginary uses for the feather. What sorts of things could it be, such as a bookmark, a quill pen, or a small duster? Be creative and think of completely imaginary things it could become, such as a feather that turns into a key, a singing feather, or an invisible pen. Write a detailed description about one of these uses. You may wish to write a story in which the main character discovers the feather and the things it can do.

Dollars and Sense! Writing Prompts

○ Imagine this is special money that never runs out. As soon as it is spent, it magically reappears in your wallet. Explain how you would spend your bill, knowing you will be able to spend only five or ten dollars at a time, but that the money will eventually reappear to be spent again.

○ Write a description of a day in the life of the bill. What do you think it would be like spending the day in a wallet, pocket, or cash-register drawer? Does the bill see interesting things, or is life boring, hot, or scary? Write from the perspective of the bill and include any thoughts or wishes the bill has as it spends a typical day.

○ You have just invented a system of money that is not paper money. Tell about the advantages or disadvantages of this system. Why would this be a better system than our current paper-bill and metal-coin currency?

○ Imagine if money were not a necessary part of our world. Write a description of how you think things would be different if people didn't need or want money.

○ Write five to ten ways money is or is not important to you or to our society. Choose one to write about in a detailed paragraph or page.

○ Write about a moment in your life when you had to deal with money in a responsible way. What did you plan to do with the money? Were you successful?

Flora and Fauna Writing Prompts

- Write a detailed description of your leaf before it is pressed and after it is pressed. Describe not only how it looks but also its texture, smell, and feel. Use lots of describing words (adjectives) so that someone who has not seen your leaf will get a clear picture of its appearance.

- Let your leaf talk! Create a dialogue between your leaf and another part of the tree, such as the trunk, or an insect. Think of and create humorous or serious topics of discussion, such as the annoyance small children cause by swinging on branches, or the problems air pollution can cause for leaves and trees.

- Write a descriptive paragraph about the sorts of things your leaf might fear. Is it afraid of fire? Of the changing seasons? Of being picked by a person? Imagine and describe things your leaf might do to help prevent some of these fears from happening.

- Compare the way a leaf looks under the microscope with what it looks like to your plain eye. Next, compare the way a leaf looks close-up in a room with the way it looks outside on a tree. Create vivid and detailed comparisons.

- Be an inventor and describe creative uses for your leaf. You can describe uses for your leaf once it is dried, such as paper. Or you can describe uses for your leaf after it has been freshly picked, such as rolled up into a drinking cup. You may also wish to invent uses for piles or bunches of leaves.

A Picture and a Thousand Words Writing Prompts

○ Choose a picture of a place that you find interesting or intriguing and glue it into your journal. Write about this picture as if you were standing there, inside the photo. Describe things such as the temperature and weather, wildlife, sounds, and any dangers that may be present. You may wish to write a story about visiting this place. Think about how you would get there and back and if it is a secret or well-known place.

○ Choose a story character you would like to invite to join you inside a picture. Write a description of what you and this character would do together in this scene. Would you explore? Would you change something about the scene? How would your character react to this scene and to being with you?

○ Find a picture of someone you would like to write about who is not famous. Create an identity for this person, describing special talents or abilities that make him or her unique, reasons why you would or would not want him or her as a friend, and one or two important life experiences this person has had. After writing your description, you may wish to write a story in which this person is the main character.

○ As you write your next story, look through magazines and find pictures of clothing, houses, toys, and other things that may belong to your story characters. Glue them in your journal and label what the items are and why they are important to your characters.

Smile! Photographs and Journals

Writing through time, descriptive writing, perspective and point of view, compare and contrast

Photographs provide a great vehicle for stimulating visual learners, providing a manageable chunk of visual information for a short descriptive piece, and encouraging narrative writing ideas.

Instant Pictures

There are several kinds of cameras that take self-developing or digital pictures that work well with the activities that follow. One in particular, the I-zone™ (by Kodak), even takes miniature self-developing pictures (2 inches by 2 inches) that fit easily in journals and are fun for students.

✔ Bring students outside or to another part of the school and allow each to take a self-developing picture. While the pictures are developing, ask students to take notes of the things in the picture that the camera may not have picked up, or things outside of the camera's eye. Since the picture will capture only a small part of the whole scene, students must "become" the camera for the rest of the scene. After pictures develop, students tape or glue them in their journals and write a complete description of what they saw that the camera didn't capture.

✔ Allow students to bring self-developing or regular film cameras outside during recess or home for the evening. Direct them to take one or two pictures of things or people they value and write about the ways this person or thing is important.

First-Day Photographs

For a twist on the traditional "first-day" photograph, take each student's picture the first week of school, but instead of displaying them, save the pictures for a month or more. Once the year is well under way, give the photographs back to students to tape in their journals. Ask them to write a descriptive page that compares how they have changed since the picture was taken. Encourage them to include descriptions of how they have changed physically and emotionally, how their friendships have grown or changed, what new things they have learned, and what sorts of things have stayed the same.

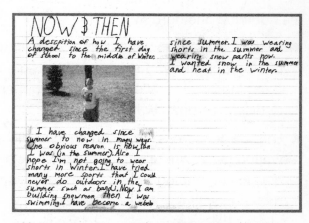

Using his first-day pictures as a reference, this student writes about how he has changed since the beginning of school.

Antique Photographs

Nearly all antique stores have boxes full of unclaimed old photographs that make great objects for students to glue or tape in journals. Either photocopy pictures or give originals to each student so they have their own. Invite students to create an identity and history for the person or persons in their picture. Questions they may wish to answer include: Who was this person? Where and when did he or she live? Who took the picture and why? What were significant accomplishments this person made? Would students like to know this person? What questions would students want to ask this person if an interview were possible?

These are 3 women who live in the 1800's. They are sisters. One is named Betty. One is named Susan and one is named Melinda. They have always lived on the prairie but they want to live in the city. But in the 1800's there wasn't a lot of money and things were different than now. So one day, they put their stuff in a wagon. They said by to their family and started off.

Provided with an antique photograph, this student begins a story about the women in the picture.

Where to Go Next: Writing Ideas • • • • • • • • • •

Use the idea of antique pictures as a starting point for writing personal histories. The Library of Congress has dozens of on-line historical interviews and photographs through their American Memory collections (www.loc.gov). Students can use the on-line American Memory interviews as the basis for creating their own interview with the person in their antique photograph.

● Instruct students to write a short essay that discusses how writing is or is not like photography. How does the writer create a picture for the reader? How is it like and unlike a photograph? How does a photographer communicate emotions in a manner similar to or different from a writer?

● Encourage students to research the culture and history of photography and create a written report about one or more aspects of photographs, such as early cameras, developing photographs or civil war photography. Reports may be displayed or students may present them orally.

Poems, Articles, and the Funny Stuff of Life
Drawing connections between writing and reading, critical analysis

The act of writing is strengthened by reading. Encourage students to become critical readers by providing short newspaper articles, poems, funny facts, or other tidbits to glue or tape in their journals.

Personal Pieces

For a critical reading and writing activity, ask students to write about a tape-in writing piece that they find meaningful. Some tape-in or write-in tidbits you can provide for students to get them started include favorite poems, goofy (yet real) laws, quirky or interesting newspaper articles, local or student newspaper articles in which your students may be featured for an accomplishment, early laws and regulations for teachers and schools. Encourage students to begin their reflection with one of the following starters:

This reminded me of…

This made me think about…

This made me wonder if…

This made me want to know more about…

If I were the author…

Some rules for teachers in 1915
 1. Can't be married
 2. must wear long skirts - no ankles showing
 3. can't wear red.
 4. can't go out after dark unless they are with their dad or brother.

I can't believe that in 1915 women teachers couldn't be married. I have had teachers who are married and they are just as good as teachers who aren't. I can't believe they had to wear long skirts too. I think that's pretty funny. Ms. Wolf doesn't even like to wear skirts!

A student reflects on some of the rules for teachers in 1915.

I set aside time to read aloud poetry to my class and to have the class read aloud poems together. We begin at one side of the room and work our way to the other side, with each student taking a turn to read one line of a poem. It is amazing how the rhythm of a poem comes through when students are providing natural line breaks by taking turns reading it. Each time we read a poem aloud in this way, the students and I discover something about the poem we may otherwise not have noticed.

3. EXTRAORDINARILY ORDINARY OBJECTS TO USE IN WRITING

Writing ideas are everywhere, waiting to be discovered. They hide in the most ordinary of objects—a lightbulb, a piece of chalk, a rock. Writing activities for students also hide everywhere, waiting to be turned into great writing projects.

In this chapter, you will find ideas and prompts that integrate "ordinary" everyday objects into interesting writing ideas and prompts for students and help make them aware of the multitude of ways writing ideas hide in our everyday lives.

Once students grow accustomed to finding writing ideas in ordinary objects, it is amazing how their writing view of the world around them changes. In a journal entry, one student wrote to me: " I never thought that a paint swatch could give you an idea for a story. That a simple pipe cleaner is a snake in disguise. Who knew a stained-glass window has a story?" I believe her words are testament to the power of helping kids unlock their imaginations.

Targeted NCTE Standards for Activities and Extensions in This Chapter:

4. Students adjust their use of spoken, written, and visual language (e.g., conventions, style, vocabulary) to communicate effectively with a variety of audiences and for different purposes.

6. Students apply knowledge of language structure, language conventions (e.g., spelling and punctuation), media techniques, figurative language, and genre to create, critique, and discuss print and non-print texts.

Can We Talk?: Interview, Reporting, and Dialogue-Writing Activities

Understanding perspective, developing characters, writing dialogue

Have students brainstorm in their journals a list of at least 20 ordinary objects for the following activities or distribute copies of A–Z Ordinary Objects to Write About (page 31) and have students fill in their own A–Z ideas. This page can be kept in student's journals as a source of writing ideas.

Interviewing and Reporting

✔ Challenge students to use their imagination and practice writing skills by interviewing an ordinary object from their list. Ask students to write their entry in an interview format, taking on the perspectives of both the interviewer and the object being interviewed. The interview should reveal at least one interesting fact or trait about the object.

✔ Have students write an eyewitness account of a unique experience an ordinary object has had. For example, what experiences has the toothbrush of a famous person had? What was it like being the quill pen used to sign the Declaration of Independence? For practice with point of view, ask students to write their account in first person, from the perspective of the object itself.

✔ Encourage students to explore and describe how different an ordinary object's life is from ours. Ask students to compare a "day in the life" of an ordinary object and a student's typical day. In what ways are they the same or different? Would students like to trade places with their object for a day? Do students think the object would like to trade places with them?

✔ For a twist on the interview format, invite students to create a play in which two or more ordinary objects are the main characters. The play might take place during a typical day in the object's life, or it might take place in the middle of the night, when the object "comes alive." Plays might also tell the life story of an ordinary object or highlight significant events in the object's life.

✔ Give students the chance to practice letter writing by writing a letter to someone from the perspective of an ordinary object. For example, an old chair might wish to write a letter to the president explaining why there should be a "National Chair Day." A lightbulb might write a letter to the electric company demanding that it get a percentage of the electrical profits since it provides the light.

> Hello, I'm a light bulb. I'm on strike because they always flick me on and off and no one ever says "thank you for lighting up this room" or "Would you like something to drink?" No, I never hear anything like that never ever, ever! So now if you don't start showing me some respect I'm going to shut off all power and you will have to be in school in the dark!

Writing as a "lightbulb," a student states her intent to go on strike.

Where to Go Next: Writing Ideas • • • • • • • • • • • • • • • •

Write on small slips of paper the names of several different objects and distribute the paper strips to students. Challenge students to write vivid descriptions about the item they have, without naming it in their writing. In small groups or as a class, invite students to read their descriptions, and let others guess which object each reader has.

A-Z Ordinary Objects to Write About and Object Interview Questions

Here are some very ordinary objects. See if you can double the list! Keep this page in your journal to help you find an object to write about. Write from one object's perspective or have a dialogue between two objects on the list.

apple core	_____	necklace	_____
bed	_____	onion	_____
chalk	_____	paper clip	_____
desk	_____	quarter	_____
egg (cooked any style)	_____	recycling bin	_____
fly trap	_____	soda can	_____
grass	_____	toothbrush	_____
hairbrush	_____	umbrella	_____
ice cube	_____	video game	_____
jelly packet	_____	window	_____
key	_____	X-ray	_____
leftovers	_____	yo-yo	_____
mud	_____	zipper	_____

Here are some questions that might help you organize an interview with and collect information about the object you've chosen.

- Where were you born?
- How long have you lived in your current place of residence?
- Do you like being _____?
- What is one secret wish you have always had?
- Describe your family.
- Have you ever wanted to be something else?

- What is your daily routine?
- Have you ever moved from one location to another? If so, how often?
- What is your definition of a "disastrous day"? What might happen on such a day?
- What kinds of things have you seen that others have not? (For example, a penny may have witnessed a bank robbery.)

Dialogue Writing

✓ Invite students to choose two items from their refrigerator and host a dialogue between them. Ask students to think about which items might have the most interesting conversations with each other and why. For example, would the mustard and ketchup strike up a conversation? What kind of issues would food in the refrigerator discuss? Would they argue? Get along? Fall in love? Feel trapped? Enjoy their lives?

✓ To help students get a feel for the ways well-written dialogue can impact writing, invite students to choose an ordinary item (see A–Z Ordinary Objects page 31 for ideas) and write a one-page story about it in which there is no dialogue at all. This story could be as simple as a "day in the life" of the object. Then ask students to keep the plot and rewrite the story, using as much dialogue as possible. Let students read aloud their entries in groups and compare as a class.

✓ Help students incorporate persuasive writing along with practice in dialogue by creating a discussion between two objects that exist in a pair (such as shoes, mittens, or arms). Through the dialogue, each object must argue why it thinks it is the more important part of the pair. You may wish to extend this to items that are typically not found in pairs but still go together, such as chalk and a chalkboard or an eraser and a pencil.

Upon hearing that dialogue can help make a story more "active," some students create incredibly long stories in which every single piece of the day is told through dialogue. The plot is lost in the minutiae of meaningless dialogue and the story gets very boring very fast. Encourage students to experiment with writing a lot of dialogue in their journals while working toward a happy medium in their stories. Point out dialogue as you read books together and discuss the ways authors use (or don't use) dialogue to tell a story.

Tip!

For young writers, the punctuation and paragraph structure of dialogue can be tricky. As students read stories, point out these things, noting that each new speaker starts a new paragraph. You may also wish to make a transparency of a page from your read-aloud book to show students its dialogue structure. Highlighting examples regularly and giving students plenty of opportunities to practice writing conversations between characters will help students better grasp the mechanics of dialogue.

Where to Go Next: Writing Ideas

To show students different ways to use dialogue in stories, compare books that don't contain much dialogue, such as Scott O'Dell's **Island of the Blue Dolphins** or Gary Paulsen's **Hatchet,** to books that have significantly more dialogue, such as Judy Blume's **Tales of a Fourth Grade Nothing** and Louis Sachar's **Holes.** Ask students to discuss the ways authors use (or chose not to use) dialogue in a story and how this changes the narrative.

A New Perspective: Ordinary Objects and Point of View

Perspective, point of view, description

How do I compare?—Comparison and Description

Ask each student to bring in a pair of interesting objects, or provide enough objects so that each student may have his or her own pair. Each student should have the same type of objects. For example, all students should have stones or each student should have one stone and one shell (see Tip for ideas). Students who need extra support can use a Venn diagram to visually organize the similar and different features of their two objects. Have students write a descriptive paragraph comparing the two objects, using vivid descriptions that compare and contrast the pair.

Ask students to gather in small groups to read and discuss their descriptions, looking for similarities and differences in the way they wrote about their objects. Encourage students to focus on the ways different individuals saw the same items. You may also wish to discuss, as a class, the ways students structured their writing so that they were able to compare items through description.

Once students are accustomed to creating descriptions of well-known objects, stretch their imaginations by providing less familiar objects, such as large plumbing washers, unusual pegs, or aquarium netting.

Tip!

I use the following common object pairs for comparison: a shell and a rock, two different rocks, pieces of fabric, differing kinds and colors of pipe cleaners, craft sticks and tongue depressors, feathers, cotton balls and cotton swabs, marbles, and straws. Lesser-known items students enjoy comparing include PVC tubes, washers, sinkers, fishing lure (without hooks!), springs, and small bolts.

Where to Go Next: Writing Ideas • • • • • • • • • • • • • • •

Every year my class writes about salt clay (recipe below), which provides a great sensory writing prompt. Each student receives a walnut-size ball and writes a description of its shape, texture, and smell. After writing descriptions, students shape their clay into a creative object of their choice, let it dry, and write stories or descriptions about this object.

Salt Clay Dough

2 cups salt

1 cup flour

1 cup warm water

SALT   FLOUR

Sift flour and salt thoroughly. Slowly knead in warm water. If dough is too moist, add flour. If dough is too dry, add water. Clay will store for several days in an airtight container. If it gets sticky, add a bit of flour. You may mix in food coloring for color. When students have shaped their pieces, allow the sculptures to air-dry for several weeks before handling.

I Can See You!—Writing Through Ordinary Perspectives

Invite the class to brainstorm a list of everyday things, such as fire, water, trees, or grass. As a class, choose one item from the list and ask students to think of different perspectives or points of view that may be associated with that item. For example, some perspectives associated with a fire might be the perspective of a firefighter fighting the fire, that of a neighbor watching the house fire, and the perspective of the person who owns the house that is on fire.

Once students have generated a list of differing perspectives, have them write a brief paragraph about the item from each different perspective. Let students share their paragraphs with the class or in small groups. Discuss how writing about the same thing changes according to the perspective. Ask students to think about the ways an author's perspective influences his or her writing and the ways the anticipated reading audience might influence a person's writing.

> Me discribing it
> smells like a fresh baked cinamin cokie.
> I feel soo delited, it feels bumby. theirs some
> white shiny iceing on it. YUM!
>
> A person straned on an island discribing it
> ohh I'm soo happy the seedweed is
> disgusting oh it smells soo good. It tasted
> like heven with the cremy iceing on it.
> the cooksie is soo yummy its Delightful
> I can't decrib the taste but I KNOW its
> good!
>
> The cookie discribing it.
> oh no I'm going in a cave OUCH! that hurt
> I'm squished I'm squised I'm to young to
> die!

A student writes about an animal cookie from three different perspectives.

Ideas for Perspectives

If students need help getting started, encourage them to write about one of the following subjects from these different perspectives:

Subject	Perspectives
Water	a farmer in drought, a person in a flood, a child playing in the rain
Piano	a teenager being forced to take lessons, a piano teacher who loves teaching, the piano strings
Animal cracker	the little kid eating it, a person with a toothache, the cracker itself
Soft carpet	a barefoot person, an ant lost in it, the vacuum cleaner
Spelling test	the teacher giving it, a student taking it, the test itself

Introducing Me...An Item's Perspective

Challenge students to write a description of themselves from the point of view of an object. For example, how would a toothbrush view them when all it sees is teeth and gums? Would it think that a human is a giant tunnel with a sluglike tongue and a cage of sharp white teeth? How would a pillow describe a person when all it sees is hair? Encourage students to brainstorm the item's perspective and provide good detail and description.

As a group activity, ask students to write an introduction of themselves from the object's point of view, read it aloud, and let others guess which object is introducing the student.

Great Literature for Brainstorming

Chris Van Allsburg's **Two Bad Ants** (Boston: HoughtonMifflin, 1988) is told without words and shows how perspective changes according to both vantage and viewpoint—in this story, from the perspective of two curious ants who decide to take a thrilling journey through a house.

Once Upon A Fairy Tale: Four Favorite Stories (New York: Viking, 2001) imaginatively presents different perspectives on four classic fairy tales. Each fairy tale is told from several view points (such as Rumpelstiltskin, the king, and the spinning wheel) and each viewpoint is read by a celebrity on the CD. Stories are illustrated by various well-known children's illustrators. The vignettes provide great models to get students started on writing from different perspectives.

Where to Go Next: Writing Ideas

Challenge students to try writing in what's technically known as third-person objective point of view. This point of view requires the writer to write as if he or she were a camera, recording the moment with no involvement of feeling. From this point of view, ask students to write about a memorable event such as a birthday party. Students should record the moment as a camera might see it. Next, encourage students to write about the same event from their own point of view (first person) and compare the two pieces.

Give students practice with perspective by asking them to choose a character from a story they are writing and describe that character from three different perspectives, such as the character's mother, the character's best friend, or the character's teacher.

Have students share their stories and let others determine from what point of view they are writing (first person or third person). Challenge them to find a way to incorporate another view point (e.g., in a third-person piece students could use a letter from another character to include first-person point of view).

Good Enough to Eat: Food-Inspired Writing Activities

Persuasive writing, writing directions, poetry

Food-Container Prompts

For a fun, quick writing prompt, use empty, clean food containers (boxes for macaroni and cheese or cereal, soda bottles, and so on) to hold sentence strips with related prompts. Photocopy and cut out the Good Enough to Eat prompts on pages 38–39 and place them in the appropriate containers. Put them in your writing center or on a table where students can easily find them and encourage students to draw one or two prompts and respond in their journals. (Have students copy and replace the prompts right away so others can use them.)

An empty cereal box provides an inviting container for writing prompts.

Tasty Descriptions

✔ Provide foods with distinctive tastes for students to try, such as very hot candies, very sour candies, or foods that students aren't accustomed to. As they are eating, ask students to take notes about what their mouth, tongue, throat, cheeks, and eyes are experiencing. Next, invite students to write a vivid description of the food in such a manner that someone reading it will feel as if he or she, too, is eating it. As a variation, provide small pieces of an appealing food (such as chocolate) and challenge students to write a description that will make someone's mouth water while reading it.

> When Mrs. Wolf unwrapped the bar I smelled a rich smell of no more hunger. The chocolate has a smooth texture to it—sweet and dark. My growling stomach is quiet now and I can still taste the sugar stuck in my teeth. I have a sticky brown spot on my fingers where the chocolate melted before it got to my mouth. Now there is a silent sound of satisfaction in the class—everyone is still savoring the dark chocolate.

A student provides a hunger-inspiring description of eating a piece of chocolate.

✔ Give students a chance to be food critics. Invite them to write a critique of a family dinner and describe such things as the atmosphere (lighting, sounds, etc.), who prepared the meal, and how it was prepared. (Provide a model of a restaurant critique from a local paper if students are unfamiliar with this format.) Challenge students to provide adequate descriptions of tastes, textures, and smells while remaining as impartial as possible.

✔ Offer students small crackers in the shape of animals. As students eat, invite students to make up the "life story" of the animal cracker, including what life has been like living among other crackers in a box. Ask students to think about what kinds of conversations crackers might have or what kinds of things they might do to pass the time in the box.

✔ Ask students to describe how three different people might perceive the same food. For example, students might compare how a baby, an elderly person, and a teenager would perceive an ear of corn. As a variation, ask students to write about one food as perceived by items, such as a garbage disposal, a blender, or an oven. Students may even wish to write from the food's perspective, such as the thoughts an ice cube has toward a freezer versus a microwave.

Tip!

Here are some foods with distinctive flavors that'll get students' mouths watering and pencils flying!

Halvah (crushed, flavored sesame seeds)
kohlrabi (a potatolike vegetable that can be eaten raw)
unusual-flavored jelly beans (hot buttered popcorn, peanut butter and jelly)
dried seaweed
stuffed grape leaves (sometimes called dolmas)
pickled foods, such as ginger, beets, watermelon rind, corn, eggs
roasted soybeans
pine nuts
edible paper (found in the novelty candy section)

Good Enough to Eat Food Prompts

Photocopy and cut out the prompts below and place them in the appropriate food containers at a writing center or other accessible spot in the classroom.

Cereal Boxes

⬤ Think of a prize that could be found in this box, hidden in the cereal. It could be real (such as the keys to a new car) or a prize that doesn't exist (such as a pet dragon). Use your imagination and write a paragraph about the prize.

⬤ Write about something someone may send away for after collecting a certain number of cereal box tops. Create a giveaway that is tangible or not tangible, such as friendship, humor, or peace, and write about how this will arrive and how it will help the receiver.

⬤ Write an interesting short story that comes in several installments, each of which may appear on a different box of cereal.

⬤ Invent and describe the ultimate breakfast cereal. Write about what shape, size, and flavor it is. Will it look like traditional cereal? For how long will it provide nutrients—a day, a week, a year? Describe how eating this cereal will affect someone.

Soda Bottles

⬤ Invent a new kind of soda. List the ingredients and create a fun new name. Write a persuasive paragraph convincing someone to try it.

⬤ Create five new uses for soda other than for drinking. For example, could it be used to power cars? Blow up balloons? Be creative!

⬤ Create several new uses for an empty soda can or bottle. Be creative and describe how these uses would help individuals or a community.

Good Enough to Eat Food Prompts (continued)

Boxed Dinners: Macaroni, Rice, Oatmeal, and More

- Write your own directions for preparing the food that came in this box. Include creative or funny things a person should say or do while cooking.

- Write a description of a creative or funny way this food will change someone's life if he or she eats it. Will it give the person X-ray vision? Superhuman strength? The ability to pass any math test?

- Imagine that the food inside this box can turn into an entire birthday or celebration feast. Write about what this celebration would look like. Who would come? What food would come from this box? What activities would take place?

- Describe the ultimate party package. What sorts of ingredients and directions are necessary for a fun party? What are the steps involved in creating the ultimate party?

- You are going to take a trip to a desert island and can bring only what fits in this box. Describe what items you would bring. Explain why you chose those specific things and why they are necessary for you.

Miscellaneous Food Containers

- Create an imaginative slogan, jingle, or persuasive paragraph advertising this product.

- Look carefully at the words used to describe this product and at the ingredients listed. Are there words you find confusing or unusual? Rewrite the product description (or ingredient list, if possible) so that it makes sense to you. You may wish to write a letter to the product company offering your suggestions.

- Create and write about the perfect snack food. Describe something that you could invent that would be small and portable, yet delicious and nutritious. What flavors would your snack come in and what name would it have?

Food Poetry

Letting students taste and experience different kinds of food provides great opportunities for poetry writing activities.

✓ One of the simplest poetry techniques is to turn descriptive sentences into free-verse poems. Without explaining that they will be writing poetry, encourage students to write a vivid sentence or two that describe beautifully the food they are eating or have eaten. Once the sentences are complete, have students rewrite their sentences as a free-verse poem. For example, they can rewrite the sentences with line breaks so that one, two, or three words fit to a line. Encourage students to read their poems quietly to themselves, stopping at each line break, and rearranging the form until it sounds rhythmic to them.

✓ Ask students to begin by writing the title of their poem in the center of the page as an adjective or as the name of the food they ate. The next line should include three words that describe the taste, look, or texture of the food. The third line should include a brief sentence stating their feelings about the food. The final line should include three words that describe the taste, texture, or look of the food, in a manner similar to line two.

✓ Challenge students to create poetry that is shaped like the food or shaped in the way it makes their mouths feel. If the food is sour, students may wish to use short, static words or lines. If the food is sweet, students may wish to create long, alluring phrases or lines.

pop, pop, pop
the popcorn
popping pop,
pop, 10, 9, 8,
7, 6 almost
done 5, 4, 3,
2, 1, done
herry, herry
eat it all
in one big
bite. Time
to make
some more.

A student constructs a free-verse poem from a descriptive sentence.

Tip!

Studies have shown that the portion of the brain responsible for writing becomes more actively involved when a person is sucking on a small piece of hard candy. To facilitate this brain "warm-up," I give students small pieces of candy before we begin writing projects and tell them to suck on the candy (not chew it), and I explain why we're doing this. Lemon has been shown to be a particularly effective flavor to help "activate" the brain before tests and projects that require higher-functioning brain activities.

Where to Go Next: Writing Ideas

Host an international food day and invite students to bring samples of traditional family foods or foods from another culture about which they want to learn. After everyone has had a chance to taste the foods, assign individuals or small groups of students to write brief descriptions of one of the foods, including who brought it and any history that person can provide about the food. Combine articles about this event (and recipes, if possible) into a class newsletter.

As a letter-writing activity, ask students to write a persuasive letter from the point of view of a food that is about to be eaten. For example, a student may write from the perspective of a piece of pizza, explaining why it thinks it should not be eaten. Is it too full of cholesterol? Is it made of "fake" cheese? Does it have a family waiting for it back in the freezer?

Writing Through the Senses

Integrating five senses into writing, comparison and contrast writing, poetry writing, descriptive writing

Senses Station Walk

The Senses Station Walk is an engaging and fun activity that integrates all five senses into writing. Students move from one sense station to another, collecting information in their journals to be used in the writing activities that follow.

Divide the class into five groups—one to begin at each of the sense stations. Allow students five to ten minutes at each station before rotating. Have groups rotate five times so that all students have the chance to stop at each station. Emphasize that students are collecting "sense" information and should take notes on what they see, hear, smell, feel, and taste, as well as on any emotions they experience.

✔ **Sound Station:** Provide a tape recorder with multiple headset jacks and play music of any of the following: nature sounds, international music, instrumental music, or other interesting forms of sound. If a multiple-jack tape player is not available, this station will work in the hall or in an adjacent room. As an alternative to music, provide a rain stick or other unusual musical instrument, such as a zither, for students to try. You can also provide simple "instruments" that students can manipulate to create sound, such as a rubber band stretched across an empty sour-cream container, or a small container filled with dried beans. Invite students to bring instruments made from things at home for others to try at the sound station. As students spend time at this station, ask them to note visual images or memories that are called up by the sounds.

✓ **Taste Station:** In small cups, provide individual samples of salt, sugar, lemon juice, small pieces of candy, soda, or other foods for students to taste. As students participate in the taste station, ask them to collect vivid, descriptive words about what they are experiencing. Encourage students to go beyond words like "bad" and "good" and use more specific words, such as "sour," "bitter," or "smooth."

✓ **Touch Station:** Provide small paper bags that contain various objects for students to feel—but not to see. Items may include raw wool (available at specialty knitting stores), fresh leaves or grass, steel wool, velvet, flour or popcorn kernels sealed in small plastic bags, rough or smooth rocks, dried and broken eggshells, feathers, candle wax, dried white glue or rubber cement, pinecones, small pieces of tree bark, sand or coffee grounds in plastic bags. As students feel items in the paper bags, encourage them to write specific descriptive phrases about textures, as well as any connections or experiences the items evoke. For example, feeling the flour in the bag may remind a student of walking in wet sand.

✓ **Sight Station:** Provide several pictures or photographs for students to study. Photographs may highlight interesting scenery or people and should be engaging in some way. *National Geographic* magazine has stunning scenic photographs that stimulate writing ideas. Old calendars are also a great source of interesting pictures or drawings. At this station, ask students to write brief descriptions of what is happening in the pictures, where the scene takes place, or why they think the pictures were taken.

✓ **Smell Station:** Fill small containers, such as empty yogurt or sour-cream cartons, with items that have distinctive smells: cinnamon, allspice, coffee grounds, unlit scented candles, scented lotion, dish soap, a small amount of perfume sprayed on a cotton ball, freshly pulled grass, lemon or orange rind, and cloves. (Remind students to take little sniffs and not inhale too deeply.)

A list of phrases and words from various "sense" stations.

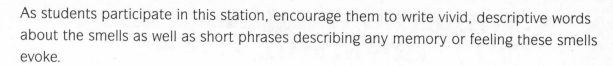

As students participate in this station, encourage them to write vivid, descriptive words about the smells as well as short phrases describing any memory or feeling these smells evoke.

✓ **Station Variation:** Instead of providing stations for each of the senses, you can focus on one sense and set up five stations that have different items related to that sense.

Where to Go Next: Writing Ideas • • • • • • • • • • •

Have students write about two or more of the senses in an integrated manner.

● Ask them to weave ideas they collected from the smell station into a description of one of the pictures they saw at the sight station. Or students may combine ideas about the music they heard at the sound station with ideas about the way things felt at the touch station and write a description about the way music "feels," literally and figuratively.

● Encourage students to combine words and phrases they collected on their station walk into free-verse poems. Invite them to mix and match words or images from several of the stations so that more than one sense is addressed in their poems.

● Hold a class discussion about how the senses are used in writing. Ask students to find examples of senses being used in picture books or chapter books. Where can students find the sense of touch? Taste? Smell? How does the use of the senses enhance or enrich the story? Discuss any ideas for stories or writing ideas students discovered on their walk. Encourage them to use these ideas for the next story they write.

● Invite students to choose an experience they have had with one of the five senses and write a short "moment in time" description of that experience. For example, a student might write about the smell of a barbecue or bonfire he attended, about the feel and texture of her dog's fur or grandmother's skin, the feel and taste of a swim in the ocean, or the sound and vibration of a movie or concert. In addition to including sensory descriptions, encourage students to add their feelings, thoughts, or opinions about the moment. Being able to vividly describe the sensations of a particular memory helps writers bring their readers into the moment of their story.

4. WALKING WITH THE PEN: WRITING SIMULATIONS

The wonderful thing about reading good stories is that they allow you to take journeys to other places without ever leaving your chair. Writing can be like that as well, allowing writers to explore and create new worlds from their imaginations. The unique stories that follow in this chapter are intended to help guide students through their own writing journeys. Each story starts with several paragraphs for students to read, then provides writing prompts, followed by a continuation of the story.

As they read and write, students must make important decisions about characters, setting, and other story elements, decisions that will affect the outcome of the story as they go. Stories act as a guided framework, allowing students to actively participate in the outcome of the story. Each framework concludes with ideas for students to continue the story or create stories of their own in the mystery or science fiction genre.

Targeted NCTE Standards for Activities and Extensions in This Chapter:

4. Students adjust their use of spoken, written, and visual language (e.g., conventions, style, vocabulary) to communicate effectively with a variety of audiences and for different purposes.

5. Students employ a wide range of strategies as they write and use different writing process elements appropriately to communicate with different audiences for a variety of purposes.

11. Students participate as knowledgeable, reflective, creative, and critical members of a variety of literacy communities.

12. Students use spoken, written, and visual language to accomplish their own purposes (e.g., for learning, enjoyment, persuasion, and the exchange of information).

Mystery: The Case of the Missing What's-It-Called

The mystery-writing simulation on pages 46–49 gives students the chance to step in as detectives and help solve a mystery. Give all students a copy of "The Case of the Missing What's-It-Called: Part 1." Ask them to read it and imagine that they are the first-person narrator and main character in the story, and respond to the questions at the end of the section in their journals. Encourage them to write imaginatively!

Prepare copies of Parts 2, 3, and 4 so that as students finish each part, they may pick up the next one. Placing sets of copies around the room will provide a small stretch break for students and help you keep track of where they are in the activity. At the end of this mystery story, students who finish early will find more ideas for mystery writing on their own.

Science Fiction: Once Upon a Time: To the Future and Back

The science fiction simulation on pages 50–52 gives students the chance to become involved in a time-travel experiment. Give all students a copy of "Once Upon a Time: To the Future and Back, Part 1." Ask them to read it and imagine that they are the first-person narrator and main character in the story, and respond creatively to the questions at the end of the section in their journals.

As in the mystery simulation assignment, have materials ready for students when they finish: Place copies of Parts 2 and 3 in an accessible spot and encourage students who finish the entire assignment early to write their own science fiction stories using the prompts at the end of Part 3.

Where to Go Next: Writing Ideas

Each genre has a distinctive "voice" that sets it apart from other genres. For example, the mystery simulation is written in the voice of a determined and curious sleuth, whereas the science fiction simulation presents the voice of an adventurer who's daring and willing to take risks. Encourage students to discuss and investigate how voice changes in the literature they've read according to audience, age of the reader, purpose of the writing, and genre.

The Case of the Missing What's-It-Called, Part 1

You have always been good at solving mysteries and everyone knows it. When something is lost you always manage to find it, and because of this, people come to you when things are missing or there is a mystery to solve. This special talent has earned you the nickname "Detective," a nickname you're proud of.

So when you woke up this morning and had a feeling it was going to be a mystery-solving kind of day, you knew that's exactly what it was going to be. Experience has told you that feeling is usually right.

After eating breakfast and saying good-bye to your folks, you pack your lunch in your backpack and head off to school, just as you would on any ordinary day.

You get to school and everything seems pretty normal. You say hello to your friends, turn in your homework, unpack your backpack. The teacher sits at her desk as usual and you start to relax a little. Perhaps no major crime has been committed. Maybe your services as a detective won't be needed after all. Everything is as it always is; normal—and that's just fine with you.

You sit down at your seat, rummage through your desk . . . and that's when you notice. Once again, that "mystery" kind of feeling you woke up with this morning was right. It is going to be that kind of day, only this time the mystery that needs solving seems to be your own. Because you can see that something is missing from your desk.

You look through your things carefully, checking under folders and under the picture you started drawing last week but didn't finish. But you can't find it. It's gone, vanished, disappeared.

In Your Journal

This is your chance to use your imagination as a word detective! Step in to the story and be part of the action. In your journal, please answer the following:

1. Describe what is missing from your desk with enough detail so that someone else can picture it.

2. Tell why this item is valuable to you. Is it valuable only to you, or does it hold value for someone else?

3. Do you have an idea of where the item might be? Who do you think might have it? Is there someone else who knows about the item and who might have taken it?

The Case of the Missing What's-It-Called, Part 2

After lunch, you head outside for a breath of fresh air. Your mind is filled with thoughts of what is missing from your desk. You are in detective mode now, and thoughts and questions bump around in your head, making it hard to think about school.

You need some time to think, to figure things out if you can. Most of the mysteries you've worked on have turned out okay. You've solved enough of them to know that there is often a simple explanation. But for some reason, this one seems a bit more challenging, maybe not as easy to solve as the others.

You walk around the playground, your mind so full you don't even notice the sounds of the other kids playing. Not today. You've got a case to solve.

You wander to your usual place on the playground where you like to go think. Things always make better sense when you're sitting here working out a case.

As you get closer, you notice something on the ground—something white, placed in the exact spot where you usually sit. Your heart beats a little faster. Could it be?

You get to the spot and reach down and pick it up. There is the missing item from your desk, wrapped in a piece of notebook paper with a rubber band around it. On the paper are these words, "Dear Detective, I have heard you are good with mysteries. I need your help with mine. I am sorry I took this from your desk but I didn't know how else to get your attention. I am very shy. Please meet me after school in the park across the street."

In Your Journal

The mystery deepens. Continue to use your imagination and create the story by answering the following in your journal. Remember, you are the main character!

1. What is your favorite place to go to think when working on a case? Describe it in detail, explaining why it is special to you and why it helps you think.

2. Is there more to the note? Are there any clues as to who wrote it (smudges of ink, fingerprints, etc)? Describe who may have written the note. Do you think it is another student? A teacher? A friend?

The Case of the Missing What's-It-Called, Part 3

The rest of the day goes by quickly. You have that tingly feeling you get when there's mystery in the air. Now that you have your missing item back, you feel better. Actually, you feel excited to meet this person and to help if you can.

The bell rings and you grab your homework and backpack and race out the door, in the direction of the park. It's a great day outside—warm but not too hot, a slight breeze blowing through the trees, birds singing. From a distance, you can see the person standing by the big tree in the middle of the park. You slow down a bit. You know the person is shy and you don't want to look scary by showing up all sweaty and out of breath. You get to the tree and introduce yourself.

In Your Journal

And the mystery person is revealed! In your journal (using your imagination of course) please answer the following:

1. Who is the person? Is it someone you know? Is it someone from your class or someone else from school? Describe him or her in detail, including hair color, eye color, clothing, and any other interesting features.

2. Describe the place where you meet. Are there other people there? Anyone who might be suspicious? Describe the sounds, sights, and smells of the park.

The Case of the Missing What's-It-Called, Part 4

You begin talking first, but soon the other person is talking, explaining the mystery. It is definitely a tough one, but you agree to take the case. You love a challenge. You whip out your notepad, which you keep with you always, and begin scribbling about what is being said, nodding every once in a while. It seems this person is also missing something, something really important. Fortunately, you are developing a plan and you know it will be no time before you can get it back. You listen for a long time, asking questions, making sure you understand the exact details of the mystery, until you realize it's time for dinner.

You turn to leave and hear "thank you." You look back and smile, knowing that once again, you are going to help someone. You turn and head home, your mind filled with thoughts of how to find the missing item. You smile, thinking of your nickname, "Detective," and happy to be on the job again.

In Your Journal

1. What is this person missing and why is it valuable to him or her? Describe it so that someone who has never seen it will be easily able to identify it.

2. What kind of plan do you have for solving the mystery? Will you be able to solve it by yourself, or will you need help from someone else? What steps will you undertake in this job?

3. Write the final scene in which you solve the mystery and return the item. How long does this take? Hours? Days? Months? Are there dangers you face along the way?

After You've Finished: Mystery Genre Writing Activities

○ Think about some of the other mysteries you have solved. Have any of your mysteries made you famous? Have any involved famous people, neighbors, teachers, friends? How have you found out about these mysteries? In what ways have people contacted you? What sorts of people have you come into contact with in dealing with these mysteries? Choose one of your favorite mysteries and write about it in story form.

○ Imagine life as a junior detective. What do you think this life would involve? Danger? Mystery? Satisfaction? What sorts of skills do you think you would need to be able to solve mysteries? Would you enjoy this life? Write a description of a week in the life of a young mystery-solving detective. You might write your description as a series of diary entries.

Once Upon a Time: To the Future and Back, Part 1

You've been best friends since you can remember, even before you started school. You have always done lots of things together and spend hours talking on the phone. So when your friend calls, you don't think too much of it. You figure it's the usual phone call wanting you to talk or go to the mall or get together or something. Your mom hands you the phone and you take it, saying, "Hi."

"You . . . You won't believe it!" Your friend sounds breathless and it's hard to understand the words.

"What? What is it?" you ask, sensing that something pretty exciting has happened.

"Just come . . . Come right now. You have to see it to believe it."

You hang up the phone, grab your jacket, and dash out the door, running all the way to the house. When you get there, your friend meets you at the door without even saying hello and drags you downstairs into the basement, to the science laboratory the two of you have spent years playing around in.

In the corner of the lab you see it. It's big, taking up the entire corner, big enough to stand inside of. You stop, staring at it with your mouth open.

"What is it?" you ask.

Your friend is excited, hopping and dancing around the thing. "It's a time machine," your friend says. "A real time machine! And it works. I already tried it!" You feel yourself being pulled into the machine. "You've got to see this!"

As you step into the machine, you grab the tool that's sitting on the workbench. For some reason you feel you should bring it along, thinking it might be useful in some way. You close the door behind you and sit down.

Your friend is at the controls and the machine starts making noises. Buttons light up, strange noises sound, and you suddenly feel very strange, a little dizzy. The machine is moving!

In Your Journal

This is your chance to become a time traveler! Imagine that you are in this story and part of the action. In your journal, reflect on the following:

1. What does the time machine look like? Did you help build it or did your friend build it alone? Describe your friend. What does he or she look like?

2. Describe what it feels like to be physically traveling in the machine. Are you scared? Excited? Both?

3. What did you take from the workbench? Describe what it looks like. Why do you think it might be helpful?

4. Where do you think you are going—the past or the future? Where would you like to go if you had a chance to be at the controls?

Once Upon a Time: To the Future and Back, Part 2

You feel the time machine slowing. There is a gentle bump, and then everything stops. Your friend looks at you and grins, saying, "Here we are. We've traveled back in time sixty-five million years."

"Sixty-five million years!" You gasp. "That's the time of the dinosaurs!"

"Yup!" Your friend continues grinning and gently opens the door of the machine.

You look out to see that the entire world has changed. There are sounds you have never heard before and creatures walking around that you have never seen before, not even in books. The air feels different, steamy and cool at the same time, and smells tangy and a little sour.

"Come on, but be careful!" Your friend is already out the door, walking down a small path that leads away from the time machine.

You step out and follow, grabbing the tool you brought from the basement.

The two of you walk for several minutes, careful not to trample anything or move anything out of place. You continue to walk, taking in all the unusual sights, until you come to a small nest of eggs.

They are the strangest eggs you have ever seen. You peer down to look more closely, noticing that they are shimmering and moving. With a gasp, you realize they are hatching!

First one cracks, then another, and another, until all six are open and you hear the tiny cries of baby dinosaurs. Suddenly, there is a tremendous shaking on the ground, and you look up and realize what kind of dinosaur eggs they are. Tyrannosaurus rex! You have just witnessed the birth of a half dozen baby T. rex, and now their mother is approaching!

"Run!" your friend screams, and the two of you take off for the time machine. You run like you've never run before, glancing over your shoulder to see the mother T. rex getting closer and closer. She is fast, but you are even faster. You are almost safe . . . but then it happens.

Your friend trips, causing you to trip, and the two of you land in a pile several feet away from the time machine. You look up to see the T. rex only feet away, and that's when you remember the tool you grabbed from your friend's basement and you know everything is going to be okay. You take action, and in a matter of a few short minutes, you are safely back inside the time machine, your friend manipulating the controls to get you both out of the past.

In Your Journal

Whew! That was close! Good thing you made it safely to the time machine. In your journal, answer the following about your adventure so far:

1. How did you use what you brought with you to get away from the T. rex and back in the time machine? Describe how your friend reacts to your actions.

2. What are two distinct things you noticed about the past? Describe at least two things you saw that were very different from the present (e.g., plants, animals, clouds, sun, etc.).

3. Where do you think you will travel next? Do you want to continue traveling through time, or have you had enough of the danger? If you could choose one other time or event to visit, which would you choose?

Once Upon a Time: To the Future and Back, Part 3

As before, you feel a bump and realize you have traveled through time again. You look at the clock to see if you're still in the past and notice that this time, you are 250 years in the future. Cautiously, you open the door and look around.

Everything is beautiful: clean, clear, and crisp. Birds sing joyously in nearby trees and the air feels warm and fresh.

Stepping out of the machine, your friend says, "So this is the future?"

Across a short field, you notice a building that looks like your school. "It can't be," you murmur. "But I think it is."

"Oh, my gosh!" Your friend sees it too. "It's our school. And it's floating!"

Sure enough, as the two of you walk toward the building you can see that the entire structure is hovering a few feet off the ground.

You approach the door and suddenly feel as if a giant hand is pushing you.

"Whoa!" your friend says, and you look over to see that the two of you have been teleported right inside the building. "Now, that's the way to travel!"

You both begin walking down the long corridor and are amazed to see the strange-looking desks and unusual ways the students are learning. Even their clothes look different.

"Hey! You there! Where are your hall passes?" A boy on a strange-looking rocket bike zips around the corner. "No passes, huh? Let's take a trip to the principal's office." He leads you down the hall and a pit of fear settles into your stomach. You look at your friend, who smiles weakly back at you, and realize you could be in real trouble here. If the principal finds

out you're from the past, you might never get back to the time machine. You might be trapped in the future forever.

An exit door hovers just down the hallway. You exchange glances with your friend. You both know what you need to do.

"Run!" you yell, and the two of you take off, diving through the door, again feeling the sensation of a hand pushing you, until you are both outside in the bright fresh sun.

"Hey!" the boy on the rocket bike calls out to you. "Hey! If you don't get back here, you're not going to be allowed to attend the Gravity Festival!"

But you can hardly hear him because you have reached the time machine. You close the door and your friend starts it up, this time set for home.

In Your Journal

1. Describe the school you were in—the furniture, the students' clothing, the unusual ways the students were learning. Does this seem like an appealing kind of school to attend? Why or why not?

2. What do you do with the time machine when you get back? Do you tell someone else about it? Destroy it? Use it again? Do you and your friend agree on what to do with it next?

After You've Finished: Science Fiction Genre Writing Activities

- If you had the opportunity to travel back in time and change one historical event, what would you change and why? What would be the consequences of this change?

- Describe a typical day in the life of a student 250 years in the future. Include descriptions of clothing, transportation, and food.

5. THE BASICS: GRAMMAR GAMES AND SKILL BUILDERS FOR JOURNALS

Say the word "grammar" to most kids and you are likely to hear loud groans. Even though it is often not a favorite subject for students, good writers must have a solid understanding of the way language works. Great writing ideas amount to nothing if you can't understand them because of poor grammar.

In this chapter, you will find journal games and activities that can strengthen students' understanding of grammar, including parts of speech and complete sentences. Each activity includes fun (and in some cases silly) examples that highlight grammar concepts. It's important that students can see that "blue," for example, is an adjective and not just the name of a color— and then use the adjective more effectively in their writing. They are more likely to learn good usage when they have a chance to play with words and see realistic, fun examples.

Students can keep activity pages and notes in a reference section in the back of their journals to refer to when they need a reminder about writing mechanics.

When students win grammar games, I let them draw prize announcement notes from our "cauldron of doom" (a big pot). Each "too good to be true" prize announcement proclaims that the student has won an unimaginably bad prize, like "a lifetime supply of toothpaste-flavored pizza." The announcements are so outrageous that students beg to pick one—and they make a great incentive. You can photocopy and cut out the prize announcements on pages 54 – 55, and then place the messages in a decorated pot or box. Besides being fun (albeit a bit strange), the prize announcements can also be used as their own writing prompts or as a review of subject/predicate, adjectives, and direct objects. Simply copy the entire page and let students cut apart the strips and sort them or use it as a worksheet.

Targeted NCTE Standards for Activities and Extensions in This Chapter:

6. Students apply knowledge of language structure, language conventions (e.g., spelling and punctuation), media techniques, figurative language, and genre to create, critique, and discuss print and non-print texts.

12. Students use spoken, written, and visual language to accomplish their own purposes (e.g., for learning, enjoyment, persuasion, and the exchange of information).

"Too Good to Be True" Prizes

You have won a year's supply of tuna-and-liver flavored ice cream!

You have won the privilege of cleaning your teacher's house for a whole month!

You are the proud owner of a dozen baby rattlesnakes!

You have won a lifetime supply of bologna-flavored oatmeal!

You have won a prized box of chocolate-covered pickled eggs!

You have won a lifetime supply of toothpaste-flavored pizza!

You have won the honor of washing your principal's car once a week!

You have won all of the spinach-flavored gelatin you can eat!

You have won a lifetime supply of onion-and-pepper-flavored gum!

You have won an invisible flea circus!

You have won an invisible brand-new sports car (it might be red)!

You have won a cake that tastes like old socks!

You have won a six-foot peanut-butter-pickle-garlic-mustard-oyster sub for lunch!

You have won a garage full of soda made out of the finest swamp water in the world!

You have won the world's largest dust bunny!

You have won your very own collection of chocolate-covered spiderwebs!

Salt and Pepper Shake-Ups: Subject and Predicate

Identification and understanding of subjects and predicates, nouns and verbs

Two empty transparent pretzel barrels make perfect "salt" (or subject) and "pepper" (or predicate) shakers for the following activity. Copy and cut out the Complete Subjects and Complete Predicates cards on pages 57–58. Put the subject and predicate cards in their respective shakers.

Student-created "salt" (subject) and "pepper" (predicate) shakers.

Divide the class into two groups—the "subject" group and the "predicate" group. Ask each student from the subject group to draw one card from the "subject" shaker and each student from the predicate group to draw one card from the "predicate" shaker.

Encourage students to circulate around the room and find a "match." If they have a subject card, they need to find a predicate card, and vice versa. Keep in mind that cards are silly and fun and do not necessarily have specific matches. Once every student is paired, partners put their cards together to make a complete sentence, making sure there is one predicate and one subject. Partners may wish to share their sentences aloud with the class and identify the simple subject and simple predicate in their sentence. After students have found one match, have them circulate again and create new sentences with new partners. Once students understand how to identify and pair subjects and predicates, ask them to write their own complete subjects and complete predicates on index cards to add to the barrels. My students enjoy this so much that by the end of the year, we usually have two full containers!

To help review predicates and subjects, choose 5–10 created sentences for students to copy into their journals, circling the subjects and underlining the predicates.

For a quick variation of the whole-class shake-up, let an individual student draw from either shaker and ask the class to write the missing part of the sentence in their journals. To make this activity even more challenging, ask students to identify the adjectives and adverbs in their sentences, as well as subjects and predicates.

Where to Go Next: Writing Ideas • • • • • • • • • • • • •

Give students the chance to play teacher by asking each to create a silly sentence, such as the ones from the activity. Compile the sentences into a single page. Copy and distribute the silly sentence sheet and ask students to identify the simple subject and simple predicate in each. You may also wish to have students identify adjectives and adverbs.

Complete Subjects

A purple spotted lizard with minty-fresh breath

The beautiful talking dog

My pencil, which just inherited a million dollars

His favorite kind of yodeling cat

Her special new singing toothpaste

A ferocious seven-headed squid

The talented young pair of scissors

His smelly old sneakers

My brand new dancing spoon

The fuzzy purple computer

The needle-spitting cactus

Her newly tuned piano

The angry bar of soap

A talking, intelligent ant

His 300-pound pair of glasses

Complete Predicates

rolled carefully across the field.

began to dance and sing an opera.

flew back to the planet Mars to visit relatives.

jumped up and ran out the door.

gave me fifty dollars to stop talking!

bought me my very own ice cream cone.

started to jump on top of my bed.

pet the cat and made it purr.

ate my entire peanut collection!

refused to stop yodeling.

asked me to dance.

made five crispy, crunchy apple pies.

took a gigantic gulp of ice-cold milk

kissed the frog right on its lips!

drove the car across the ocean.

Around the World in Ten Minutes: Parts of Speech

Identifying nouns, verbs, adjectives, adverbs

Ask students to open their journals to a blank page and stand in front of their desks. Using the prompt list on page 60, call out a prompt such as, "Name your favorite dessert," and ask students to write a response in their journals. Do not tell students what part of speech the prompt asks for.

Now ask students to write their response in the journals of three to five other students. (This will require them to move around the room as well as to treat other students' journals with respect.) Students may not duplicate something that has already been written in response to the same prompt. After students have written in several journals, call out a new prompt from another part of speech. As you continue, check to see that students are circulating so that all journals are written in. Select prompts in a random fashion from each of the four parts of speech.

Once students have written 10 to 20 prompts in different journals, invite them to return to their seats. Ask them to turn to a new journal page, turn the journal horizontally, and place the headings *noun, verb, adjective,* and *adverb* across the top. Then direct students to sort their lists, rewriting words in the proper category. Let students work with partners if they need support with identifying parts of speech.

A student collected parts of a speech from other students. He circled the nouns and put a box around the verbs. Next, he will sort them into list form.

Great Literature for Brainstorming

A Cache of Jewels by Ruth Heller (New York: Grosset and Dunlap, 1987) is a richly illustrated, lyrical book about collective nouns that will keep students turning the pages—and engage them with grammar. Ruth Heller has written several books that feature different parts of speech. Look also for **Kites Sail High** (verbs), **Many Luscious Lollipops** (adjectives), and **Merry-Go-Round** (nouns). Read aloud the book that matches the part of speech you wish to review and then place the book in a language center for students to return to for reinforcement. Students might also make illustrated reference posters based on Heller's work that provide examples of each part of speech. Display them around the classroom where students can refer to them easily.

Around the World Prompts

Nouns

Name an animal that most people would not want to have as a pet.

List your favorite fast-food restaurants.

Name your favorite dessert.

List things you might find in a secret treasure chest.

Name your most favorite vehicle.

Verbs

List things to do on a vacation.

Name things to do in the water.

List things to do with food (besides eat it).

Name things to do with your arms or legs.

List things you would do if you had $1,000.

Adjectives

List your favorite color(s).

Name the way an animal's fur or skin can feel.

List kinds of temperature or types of weather.

Name words to describe food (amusement rides, homework, school).

List the way a kitchen might smell.

List an age you think is old.

Write a number between _____ and _____.

Adverbs

Describe how a person might watch TV (or cook, sing, eat, laugh).

List words that describe how you move when you play your favorite hobby or sport.

List words that tell how or when you wake up.

Describe how you would talk to be heard in a noisy cafeteria during lunch.

Describe how you might feel before a test (on a ride, during a holiday).

Where to Go Next: Writing Ideas • • • • • • • • • • • • • • • • •

Create a large class chart of favorites in each category—noun, verb, adjective, and adverb—that can serve as a friendly way to help students remember specific parts of speech. As students find their own special words, invite them to add these words to the class list.

Ask students to pick a number between 3 and 6, look back at their original Around the World lists, and choose the same number of things from different categories. Challenge students to combine all of those words into one sentence, adding their own words as needed. Invite students to share their sentences with the class, and have other students identify the parts of speech in the sentence.

Discuss how using vivid words can help make students' writing more interesting. As a class, choose several overused verbs (e.g., *run, eat, said*) or adjectives (e.g., *pretty, fun, nice*) and ask students to brainstorm vivid synonyms for these words. Collect their responses on a class-size poster or have students keep individual collections in their journals. Look through picture books, sports articles, and read-alouds for vivid verbs and adjectives.

Keeping It Basic: Parts of Speech
Identifying nouns, verbs, adjectives, adverbs

The parts of speech cards on page 62 can be copied onto card stock, cut apart, and used in many ways, including as a sorting activity at a language-arts center. To introduce the class to the card activity using their journals, distribute the cards evenly to students without telling them which part of speech each is. Invite students to circulate around the room, discussing with each other what part of speech they have, and forming groups of four so that each part of speech is represented. If you don't have the right number of students to make even groups of four, let some groups take an additional member, so that one part of speech is represented twice.

Once all students are in groups, challenge each group to create a sentence using the words from their cards. Encourage creativity and imagination and invite groups to present their sentences to the class. When students understand how this activity works, let them circulate several times and create new sentences and groups.

Great Literature for Word Study

Frindle by Andrew Clements (New York: Aladdin, 1998) offers students a chance to understand the way we attach meaning to words. When the main character decides to change the name for "pen," and renames it "frindle," this small act sparks a large chain of events. Have students write a journal entry about a topic such as all the things a kid can do on a snow day, without using the noun "snow"—let them create a nonsense noun to use in its place. Challenge students to try this with other parts of speech as well.

At the end of the grouping activity, have students write their favorite group sentence in their journals and use it as a jumping-off point for a journal entry.

Where to Go Next: Writing Ideas

Help students practice writing paragraphs by inviting them to take their best created sentence and use it as a topic sentence for a descriptive paragraph. Remind students that a well-crafted paragraph has sentences that support the topic sentence. Because of the nature of the words, paragraphs might be humorous but should still make sense. Invite students to draw pictures to accompany their paragraphs and share their work with the class.

Let students look through newspapers and magazines and make their own parts of speech word cards. Invite them to cut the words out, glue them on small pieces of tagboard, and keep them in a container for the class to use. Discuss which parts of speech are easiest to find in print. Is it easier to find nouns or verbs? Are adverbs or adjectives used more in magazines and newspapers? Challenge students to look for one part of speech and list as many examples as they can find in print, in 10 minutes.

Parts of Speech Cards

Nouns

snow	marshmallow
bubble gum	frog
toothpaste	paper clip
crocodile	teeth
pencil	lightbulb

Verbs

ran	jumped
hid	flew
ate	sank
dodged	drank
scrubbed	talked

Adjectives

soft	hairy
tall	round
dusty	clear
fat	blue
scary	tiny

Adverbs

slowly	fearfully
boldly	merrily
proudly	quickly
carefully	wickedly
cheerfully	bravely

6. FABULOUSLY FREE WRITING FIELD TRIPS

Field trips can be great fun for students. They offer the chance to learn in a completely different setting outside the traditional classroom. Field trips can also be expensive for students (not to mention stressful for teachers!).

In this chapter, you will find opportunities for free field trips your class can take in and around your school, using the journal as your bus—no permission slips required! Using their journals and powers of observation, students will practice writing skills in description, comparing and contrasting, and perspective.

Here are some places to take your writing field trips:

the playground	music room	nurse's office
library	school office	custodial room
gym	parking lot	computer lab
cafeteria	auditorium/theater	
hallway	science lab	

You might even arrange a visit to "observe" another classroom.

Targeted NCTE Standards for Activities and Extensions in This Chapter:

4. Students adjust their use of spoken, written, and visual language (e.g., conventions, style, vocabulary) to communicate effectively with a variety of audiences and for different purposes.

5. Students employ a wide range of strategies as they write and use different writing process elements appropriately to communicate with different audiences for a variety of purposes.

11. Students participate as knowledgeable, reflective, creative, and critical members of a variety of literacy communities.

12. Students use spoken, written, and visual language to accomplish their own purposes (e.g., for learning, enjoyment, persuasion, and the exchange of information).

Perspective/Compare-and-Contrast-Writing Field Trips
Point of view, perspective, compare and contrast

On this field trip, students practice looking at and writing about contrasting perspectives in various places around your school. Choose one of the places below and bring students, with journals in hand, to that location. Ask students to collect sights, sounds, and impressions from this place. Encourage students to make at least 10 different short notes of sensory impressions or experiences. Return to the classroom and ask students to reread their notes and write briefly about the place. How did they see or experience this place and the objects in it? Next, ask students to write about this place from a different perspective, using the suggestions below.

Outside the Cafeteria (around lunchtime)

After visiting the cafeteria, encourage students to write contrasting paragraphs that address how a person might feel standing by the cafeteria in the following situations: He or she hasn't eaten all day, is completely stuffed, or has the flu. As a variation, invite students to write first-person descriptive paragraphs comparing how a table, the cafeteria floor, or a cook might experience this place.

In or Near the Science Lab

After collecting notes in or near the science lab, ask students to write at least two first-person contrasting paragraphs describing how any of the following might experience the science lab: a guinea pig (or other animal in the lab), a microscope, a test tube, the lab sink, or safety goggles. Encourage students to find their own objects from the science lab from whose perspectives they can write.

In or Near the Music Room

After collecting written notes in or near the music or band room, invite students to write at least two first-person contrasting paragraphs describing how any of the following might experience this room: the piano bench, the piano keys, a musical instrument, a music book, or a conductor's baton.

School Hallways or Entryways

Spend a few minutes allowing students to collect notes in one of the school's hallways or near the school entrance and write at least two first-person contrasting paragraphs describing how any of the following might experience these areas: a door to the outside, a bird looking in from the outside, a locker, the ceiling, a poster on the wall, a fire alarm pull, or the floor.

Playground

Outside, encourage students to collect notes and write at least two first-person contrasting paragraphs describing how any of the following might experience the playground: gravel or asphalt, swings or other playground equipment, playground toys such as basketballs or jump ropes, or a nearby plant or tree. For variety, invite students to write descriptions of the same subject as it or its environment changes over the course of the year.

Classroom

In your own classroom, encourage students to collect notes and write at least two first-person contrasting paragraphs describing the experiences of any of the following: the teacher's desk, their own desk, chalk, a poster, the chalkboard, a student's pencil, or a plant.

> I walked to my spot at the cashier's place. The first class came in to the cafetiria. A boy who looked like he was from 1st grade with glasses and boatloads of freckles had to wake me up. "I hate this job", I thought.
>
> "Wham!" A humming kid sat down on me with crackers and pop. I knew what was going to happen. The kid set down his crackers, then he slam his pop can down on my head, hard. Dazed, I thought bitterly, "There go another 10 brain cells — no, chair cells!"
>
> "Wham!" Another kid came down on me. He didn't have pop. Thank Goodness! The two kids started chattering. Soon, the whole cafeteria was roaring and thundering with voices. Finally, it was night!

During a writing field trip, this student describes the cafeteria from the perspective of a clerk serving food and from the perspective of a table.

Where to Go Next: Writing Ideas • • • • • • • • • • • • • • •

Lead a discussion about character perspective. Ask students why it is important to be able to write from different perspectives. How does this change writing? Does it make it more interesting? How do writers blend their own (and differing) perspectives into their writing? You might take two published models that use very different perspectives and contrast them. **A View From Saturday** by E. L. Konigsburg tells one story from several different viewpoints. **Tales of a Fourth Grade Nothing** by Judy Blume tells a story from the character of Peter Hatcher, whereas Blume's **Otherwise Known as Sheila the Great** tells a story through the eyes of a classmate of Peter Hatcher, offering a completely different perspective from his.

For homework, ask students to write about a walk through their house from the perspective of an ant, as in Chris Van Allsburg's **Two Bad Ants** (see page 35). How would an ant's view of their house compare to their own view of it? What kind of dangers and perils would it find?

Eyes and Ears: Descriptive-Writing Field Trips

Descriptive writing, compare and contrast

This activity helps students understand the importance of integrating visual and auditory details into writing. Begin by darkening your classroom. Ask students to spend two minutes focusing closely on the sounds of your classroom and school, paying attention to how things sound and feel different when the room is quiet and dark. With the lights back on, ask students to list all the things they heard or noticed. Encourage them to write a descriptive paragraph about the classroom that focuses only on the sense of hearing. What is the experience of the classroom through their ears only? How is it different from experiencing it with their eyes? Then ask students to write a descriptive paragraph that focuses mainly on the sense of sight. Discuss what is missing from a description when the writer focuses on only one sense.

As a variation, take your class (with journals) to different places in the school, such as a hallway, the library, in or near the cafeteria, near the gym, or outside on the playground or school grounds. Encourage students to collect information about this place using their eyes for one minute and then their ears for one minute, and write contrasting paragraphs about their experience of the same place through different senses.

If your school is hosting an event such as a science fair or a book fair (or there is construction nearby), take advantage of this and bring your students near the action to collect information for descriptive "eyes or ears" paragraphs.

Where to Go Next: Writing Ideas • • • • • • • • • • • • • •

Encourage students to find examples of each of the senses as they are used in writing. Look for examples in poetry, magazine articles, newspaper articles, and books. Discuss how the writing sample would change without the integration of the sense or senses the author chose. Then, using the examples they've found as models, invite students to write a page describing a place so that someone else can see or hear it. Places to write about may include their house, a shopping center, an amusement park, a farm or zoo, or a museum. Ask students to share and compare the differences in "seeing" a place versus "hearing" a place. If possible, ask students to think of places they could describe through the sense of smell or touch and compare in a similar manner.

Use this activity as practice for students to integrate into larger writing projects. For your next expository, persuasive, or narrative project, challenge students to integrate at least one sense in one place in their writing so that the reader receives more of a three-dimensional experience. Encourage students to include senses other than sight, which is often the sense young writers rely on most.

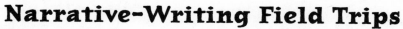

Narrative-Writing Field Trips

Real-life connections to writing, narrative writing, cultivating imagination

Imagination Story Starters

Writers are often asked where they get their ideas. Use this activity to help show students that writing ideas are everywhere. With journals in hand, invite students on a walking field trip in and around your school. Ask them to look for things they see every day that could be mixed with imagination to become interesting story possibilities.

When I taught second grade, each student decorated his or her own pair of "imagination glasses" made out of short cardboard tubes (toilet paper roll cores work well) glued together to look like binoculars. We took our glasses on walking field trips, and students knew that when they looked through them, they would see things that you couldn't see without your imagination. My students absolutely loved going on these imagination walks, and I was amazed at the things the kids "saw" through their glasses. Although older students may find this silly, if you have younger classroom "buddies," your class may wish to make imagination glasses to share with their buddies. Older students can elicit imaginative details from their younger buddies and can help record them in the buddy's journal.

For example, a row of lockers may become an army of statues waiting quietly. A large entry hall may become a cave with ice crystals hanging down from the ceiling. An outside portable classroom may become a castle or a secret hideaway. A large hill outside may be a volcano ready to erupt at any moment.

Back in the classroom, encourage students to share ideas with each other and keep a list in their journal to refer back to for story ideas. Ask students to choose one and weave it into a story.

Narrative-Writing Prompt Mini-Journeys

Help students develop imagination as they travel to various places in your school with the writing prompts found below. Make multiple copies of the prompts on page 68, cut them out, and put them into envelopes. Bring students to each corresponding location, give them the appropriate sentence strip, and ask them to respond to the prompt in their journals. Let students know that they will likely not have a chance to finish stories but will have many starts or ideas for several to finish later.

Narrative-Writing Mini-Journeys

Playground:
She was all alone when I found her and offered to be her friend.

Library:
It looked like an ordinary book. But instead of pages inside, I found a large brass key.

Gym:
Suddenly, I could run faster than ever, and I knew it had something to do with the shoes I found.

Cafeteria:
Before we knew what happened, the whole place was filled with growing vines and trees. We were in a rain forest.

Hallway:
There it was, at the end of the hall, a small door I had never noticed before.

Music Room:
When I got closer, I saw that the violin was playing by itself.

Parking Lot:
The car looked like any other car, until I watched it lift off the ground and begin to fly.

Auditorium/Theater:
Suddenly, the lights went out and I could tell I was no longer alone.

7. STORY STARTERS AND WRITING PROMPTS

Sometimes, the hardest part about writing stories and essays can be getting started. For young writers, often all that is needed is the beginning of an idea—and then they are off and writing.

In this chapter, you will find both narrative and nonfiction writing prompts designed to help students jump-start their writing. The prompts can be used as a warm-up writing activity or as assignments in their own right.

Targeted NCTE Standards for Activities and Extensions in This Chapter:

4. Students adjust their use of spoken, written, and visual language (e.g., conventions, style, vocabulary) to communicate effectively with a variety of audiences and for different purposes.

5. Students employ a wide range of strategies as they write and use different writing process elements appropriately to communicate with different audiences for a variety of purposes.

6. Students apply knowledge of language structure, language conventions (e.g., spelling and punctuation), media techniques, figurative language, and genre to create, critique, and discuss print and non-print texts.

11. Students participate as knowledgeable, reflective, creative, and critical members of a variety of literacy communities.

12. Students use spoken, written, and visual language to accomplish their own purposes (e.g., for learning, enjoyment, persuasion, and the exchange of information).

Paragraph and Sentence Story Starters

Narrative writing

The story starters on page 71 are designed to be used in a variety of ways. You can give them as individual prompts to help students get started on their own stories. Or you may wish to use the prompts for a group writing activity, in which each student writes to one prompt for a designated amount of time and then passes his or her story to a neighbor to continue. Each story can be passed along to a number of different students, and finally returned to the original owner to finish. This activity teaches students about writing voice and the way that different writers' perspectives influence the same piece of writing.

Offer students who need more support the paragraph story starters. You may also want to have the class respond to one prompt as a group, with all students contributing as you write the beginning of the story on the overhead or on chart paper. Allow pairs or individuals to finish the ending.

Where to Go Next: Writing Ideas . . . .

Include one or two story starters in a class notebook that students can check out and take home for a weekend. Invite family members (and students themselves) to continue the stories while they have the notebook at home. Younger family members may wish to add drawings to the notebook. This story notebook can become part of your fiction library.

Assign the entire class to write one page using the same prompt. In small groups, ask students to share what they have written and discuss the ways different authors wrote about the same prompt. Ask students to discuss how different perspectives and writing voices changed the same prompt.

Nonfiction Writing Prompts

Descriptive writing, compare and contrast

The nonfiction prompts on page 72 can be used in a variety of ways. Post one daily on the board or compile several into a list for students to keep in their journals to use for free-writing time. Send a few home weekly as at-home writing inspirations. Assign certain prompts as compare-contrast or descriptive essays. For additional nonfiction writing prompts, look at the dice activities on pages 13 and 14.

Story Starters

Paragraph Story Starters

● I was in my room trying to find my favorite shoes in my closet. I opened the door and began looking when I noticed something I had never seen before. In the back wall of my closet was a tiny door with a shining golden doorknob. Where had it come from and what was it doing in the back of my closet? I . . .

● At last the package I had ordered three months ago arrived. I practically tore it away from the mail carrier and flew down the stairs to my bedroom. Eagerly, I opened the box and stared. There it sat, just waiting for me to put it together and get started. That was when I noticed . . .

● Once again, I got stuck doing the dishes while my little sister got to watch TV. She was in the family room and I was in the kitchen, washing away, looking out the window, when I saw him. He was a tiny man in our backyard and he was digging. I put the dishes down, soapsuds and all, and peered into the dark. I wasn't sure I could believe my eyes. Was I really seeing what I thought I was seeing?

● I hadn't meant for anything weird to happen with my new chemistry set. I was just playing around, mixing this and that, when suddenly there was a loud "poof," a wisp of smoke, and a smell like cinnamon. I looked around and everything seemed okay. But when I looked in the mirror . . .

Sentence Story Starters

● My hiccups were so bad my teacher sent me to the hall to get a drink. But when I turned on the faucet, it wasn't water that came out.

● There we were, locked in the school library for the night.

● I couldn't tell at first what kind of creature it was. I just knew it needed my help.

● Who would have thought the ugly old thing I found would turn out to be a lost treasure?

● I had just sat down at the computer to work on my report when the keys suddenly started going crazy.

Super-Quick Story Starters

● Just when I thought it was over, it . . .

● The best day of my life was . . .

● How was I to know the whole thing was going to be ruined when . . .

● She was the meanest person I knew until. . .

● I knew I couldn't keep the dog a secret much longer . . .

● I wouldn't have opened the secret letter I found, but . . .

Nonfiction Prompts

What-if Prompts

- If you could have a conversation with any character from a book, who would you choose and what would you discuss?

- If bugs could talk, what would you want to ask? Would you want to tell or ask bugs anything?

- If the place where you live could talk, what kind of stories would it tell? Is there one part of the home that would have more to say than the others? Would there be complaints? Stories about previous owners?

- If you had a choice between being invisible or being able to fly, which would you choose and why? Which do you think would be better?

- If you were in charge of the whole world for an entire day, what would you do?

- If you could spend a week observing one historical moment in the past, what would you choose and what would you do while you were there?

- How do you envision your life ten years from now? Twenty years? Fifty years?

- Create the ultimate bedroom for yourself. The sky is the limit. Would yours include a swimming pool? Tropical rain forest? Movie theater? Ice hockey rink?

- If you could live for a week with an animal in the wild, which animal would you want to live with? What would you do? What do you think you would learn?

- What do you like about being a kid? What do you look forward to about becoming an adult? Do you think one is better than the other? Why or why not?

- What would you do if you could stop time for five hours?

It's-a-Fact Prompts

- The average human needs 7–8 hours of sleep each night to stay healthy. How would life be different if we didn't need sleep? If we lived for 500 years? Would life be better or worse? Why?

- Earth is a sphere that rotates on an axis and revolves around the sun. What if most people still believed Earth was flat? Would you try to convince them otherwise? Would you attempt to prove that it is not? How?

- Humans have explored the moon and landed space vehicles on Mars. Which planet would you visit in our solar system if space travel were possible there?

- If you lost the ability to use one of your five senses, you would likely develop stronger sensitivity in the other four senses. Write a letter to a person who is blind, describing the sunset, a rose garden, a forest, the colors of your favorite blanket, yourself. Write a letter to a person who is deaf, describing music, a waterfall, birds singing, the doorbell. Use the four senses that you share with this person to help him or her experience the place or thing about which you're writing.

8. THE JOURNAL AS A TOOL FOR BUILDING CLASSROOM COMMUNITY

In a way, each of your students is like an individual piece of the classroom "puzzle," fitting together with others in the class community through your guidance.

Even though journals are, by nature, individualistic, they make excellent vehicles for building class community. The section that follows offers activities that help students get to know each other better, while building a sense of common purpose and community in your room. In addition, students have the chance to explore who they are as writers and to appreciate and learn from the other writers around them.

Targeted NCTE Standards for Activities and Extensions in This Chapter:

5. Students employ a wide range of strategies as they write and use different writing process elements appropriately to communicate with different audiences for a variety of purposes.

6. Students apply knowledge of language structure, language conventions (e.g., spelling and punctuation), media techniques, figurative language, and genre to create, critique, and discuss print and non-print texts.

9. Students develop an understanding of and respect for diversity in language use, patterns, and dialects across cultures, ethnic groups, geographic regions, and social roles.

(For classes with English language learners) 10. Students whose first language is not English make use of their first language to develop competency in the English language arts and to develop understanding of content across the curriculum.

11. Students participate as knowledgeable, reflective, creative, and critical members of a variety of literacy communities.

12. Students use spoken, written, and visual language to accomplish their own purposes (e.g., for learning, enjoyment, persuasion, and the exchange of information).

Dear Teacher

Letter writing

You can learn some amazing things about students by asking them to write you personal letters in their journals. Each week, choose approximately five different students to write you a letter. Encourage students to write about anything—what is happening in their lives, what is happening at school, or questions they want to ask you. Collect journals on Friday and write a return letter in the journals to be delivered on Monday. With this system, every child will have the chance to write and receive a letter each month.

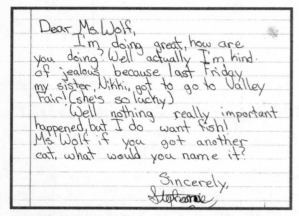

A written interaction between student and teacher.

Compliment List

Tone and audience

Everyone likes to hear compliments. And compliments are even more powerful when they are written. For this community-building activity, ask students to write their name at the top of a blank page in their journal and leave it open on their desk. Ask students to circulate around the room in a predetermined fashion and write something they like about each person in his or her open journal. If you are concerned that students will copy what others have written (one student receives 25 "I like your smile" compliments), have students place a privacy piece of paper on top of the list so that all other compliments are covered. Encourage students to think about personal traits they admire in their peers that are about personality and actions rather than appearances.

Sometimes kids who are shy in class have opened up to me through their journal letters and I have learned things about them I might not have known without the opportunity for this private form of communication. Besides letters, students have included poems and pictures, all of which have helped me get to know and understand them better. As busy as teaching can be, I have found that taking the time to read and respond to student letters is well worth the effort.

As a class, keep track of compliments received for whole-class behavior in other parts of the school for things such as quiet hall behavior, nice lunchroom manners, or playground courtesy. Ask students to notice and point out other classes who are behaving in a positive manner. You may wish to have all students keep track of compliments on a designated journal page, assign a "secretary," or create a class compliment poster that everyone can see.

Periodically, provide writing prompts for students regarding compliments. Encourage students to write about any of the following: How does it feel to give and receive compliments? Can it be difficult to accept compliments? If so, why? Do you feel compliments are important—why or why not?

Planting a Community
Writing to record data, descriptive writing

Growing a class plant offers the opportunity for community building within your classroom as well as an outreach community project, teaching students about both writing and recording scientific data.

Need a source for seeds? See Resources, page 80.

A number of houseplants (such as coleus) grow well from seed and a number of plants (such as philodendron and purple passion) grow well from cuttings. All are easy to care for. Before planting, ask students to reserve a few pages in their journal for data recording and in that section write a brief paragraph about what they think the plant will look like when it first sprouts and when it is full grown.

Next, invite each student to plant his or her own seed or cutting in a small seedling cup or small glass of water. Weekly, ask students to add written data entries about the plant in their reserved section. Remind students that their entries, like those of scientists, should be objective, but may include their thoughts and musings. Assign groups or individual students to be responsible for the plants as they grow. Once seedlings are large enough, transplant them into larger pots so that eventually your class will have two or three full-grown plants.

In addition to collecting data about plants, you may wish to provide students with some of the writing prompts that follow. As your plants grow, help students understand that your class is a community working together to care for the plants and that they will pass that caring on to the larger community at year's end by giving the plants away.

At the end of the year, vote as a class on who in the community should receive the plant, such as a nursing home, someone's sick relative, a fire station, a vet's office, etc.

Some prompts to incorporate in your planting-writing activities include

- What if we could invent a plant that eats garbage?

- How are plants important to people? To Earth? To animals?

- What does it mean to be responsible? To work in groups? To cooperate?

- What is a community? Is a sense of community automatic, or do you have to work to create it?

> Plants are really important for a lot of reasons. They make things pretty and the leaves add oxygen to the air. They make homes for animals. The wood from trees makes homes for people to. Sometimes plants are used for paper for students in schools. I like plants. I'm glad they are here.

A student shares her thoughts about the importance of plants.

Great Literature for Writing About Nature

The Plant That Ate Dirty Socks by Nancy McArthur (New York: Avon Books, 1988) is an engaging chapter book about two unusual plants that eat dirty socks. Although it is geared toward younger students (grade 3), it is a fun read that provides a nice literature link with growing a class plant. Students enjoy McArthur's humor and the book can be used as a springboard to writing about our environment and the role of plants in our lives.

Character Pen Pals
Characterization, letter writing

Participating in the character pen pal activity allows students to use their imaginations and "become" someone else for a while. As students write to one another in the guise of other characters, they get to see one another in a creative, new light.

Begin by asking students to create in their journals a character with an identity different from their own. The identity description should include the character's age, gender, name, occupation, hobbies and spare-time activities, location of residence, one secret wish, favorite food, and favorite book.

Next, on a clean journal page, ask students to write a letter as the character they created, introducing themselves to a pen pal and including at least three character details about their made-up identity. Students should also ask at least one question that their pen pal can answer.

Have each student copy over the letter neatly and fold it or place it in an envelope with the initials of their given names in one of the corners. You will facilitate the exchange of the letters so that each student receives a letter from another "character." This exchange will initiate the pen pal relationship between student partners who are writing and responding "in character"—a partnership that will continue through the week or through the year.

Tip!

Although this may feel a bit strange to students at first, once they understand how it works, They really let go and get creative with their letter exchanges. When writing as someone different, students may feel free of typical roles they have in class. I have even had students branch out on their own with this activity and exchange character pen pals within friend groups.

To keep the identities of student authors secret (which adds to students' enthusiasm for the activity and incorporates problem-solving skills as they attempt to guess the identity of their character pen pal), have students type their letters. Give a number or code to each student, which they will write on their letter. Make a list of pen pal pairs using students' codes and then write the real name of the recipient on each letter.

After letters have been delivered, instruct students to read them and write back, in the identity of their character. Remind students to write their codes on the top of their letter so you can facilitate the exchange again. Students may inadvertently find out who their pen pal is, but encourage them to continue writing "in character" as long as the activity lasts. At the end of the activity, give students two chances to guess the identity of their character pen pal. Then let students reveal their true identities to one another.

Mystery Box
Critical thinking, compare and contrast, descriptive writing

The mystery box is a great way to combine problem solving, writing, and community building into one activity. The box itself can be any empty box that students decorate with paper question marks. Once a week, choose a new student to be the "mystery box person"—the person who is responsible for deciding what item will be "placed" in the box. The item must be something real but will not actually go into the box and does not have to be small enough to fit in the box. You may use The Mystery Box! reproducible on page 79 as a guide for this.

At the beginning of the week, ask the mystery box person to write a paragraph description about his or her item, including its color, size, shape, and texture, and place it inside the box. Each day during the week, invite the rest of the class to ask up to 10 questions that can be answered yes or no to deduce what's in the box, such as, "Do we use it during school hours?" One student may act as recorder to keep track of what the class has learned about the object. At the end of a week, if students have not guessed, the mystery box person reveals the object by reading his or her description of it.

Students will quickly catch on to the type of questions that need to be asked. Initially, they may just try to guess the item without first narrowing down its descriptors. Guide them with the questions below if necessary.

Questions to Guide Guessing

Is it alive?

Is it intended for children? For adults? For both?

Can it fit in the box?

Is it edible? (Would someone want to eat it?)

Is it something familiar to all children?

Is it something useful?

Is it something to play with?

Here are some ideas students have used for the mystery box item: computer virus, flag, the continental United States, hockey stick, baseball, button, license plate, checkbook, driver's license, a hat, an atom, a piece of candy or gum, Mars, a leopard, a can of soda.

Where to Go Next: Writing Ideas ● ● ● ● ● ● ● ● ●

Before beginning to guess, have each student write a paragraph in his or her journal about the mystery box person. Explain that describing the classmate may provide clues about what he or she chose to put in the box. After the item has been guessed, check to see if anyone found a connection between the student's personality and his or her mystery box item.

The Mystery Box!

Name _____

I am in charge of the mystery box the week of _____

My item is_____

Directions: Please write at least one paragraph describing your item. Make sure to include the color, size, shape, and other important details about your item. Remember, your readers should be able to "see" your item from your description! Use the detail list at the bottom of the page to help you.

_____

_____

_____

_____

_____

_____

_____

_____

_____

Detail Checklist (Include at least three of these characteristics in your paragraph):

_____ shape   _____ smell   _____ personality

_____ size   _____ sound   _____ where it stays most of
                                                the time
_____ color   _____ temperature
                                          _____ what it's used for
_____ texture   _____ age

_____ taste   _____ weight

RESOURCES

INTERNET SITES

American Library Association
www.ala.org/alsc/teachers.links
Dozens of language-arts links for teachers that include theory, issues,
lesson plans, children's literature, and many others.

National Council of Teachers of English
www.ncte.org
Specifically designed for English teachers and offers links and information regarding national
literacy standards and current literacy issues.

The Children's Literature Web Guide
www.ucalgary.ca
An amazing number of ideas and links for read-aloud books that can be incorporated into
journal activities, as well as general information about children's literature and literacy
education, including a comprehensive list of current children's authors with corresponding
links.

International Reading Association
www.reading.org
Information and links regarding literacy and the teaching of reading in education today,
including lesson plans for writing.

MISCELLANEOUS

Overhead Dice (for Roll 'Em . . . List Activities with Dice, page 13)
EAI Education
1-800-770-8010
www.eaieducation.com

Seed Distributors (for Planting a Community, page 75)
Park Seed
1-800-845-3369
www.parkseed.com

Burpee Seeds
www.burpee.com